History of Germany

An Enthralling Overview of Major Events and Figures

© Copyright 2024 - All rights reserved.

The content contained within this book may not be reproduced, duplicated, or transmitted without direct written permission from the author or the publisher.

Under no circumstances will any blame or legal responsibility be held against the publisher, or author, for any damages, reparation, or monetary loss due to the information contained within this book, either directly or indirectly.

Legal Notice:

This book is copyright protected. It is only for personal use. You cannot amend, distribute, sell, use, quote, or paraphrase any part, or the content within this book, without the consent of the author or publisher.

Disclaimer Notice:

Please note the information contained within this document is for educational and entertainment purposes only. All effort has been executed to present accurate, up-to-date, reliable, and complete information. No warranties of any kind are declared or implied. Readers acknowledge that the author is not engaging in the rendering of legal, financial, medical, or professional advice. The content within this book has been derived from various sources. Please consult a licensed professional before attempting any techniques outlined in this book.

By reading this document, the reader agrees that under no circumstances is the author responsible for any losses, direct or indirect, that are incurred as a result of the use of the information contained within this document, including, but not limited to, errors, omissions, or inaccuracies.

Free limited time bonus

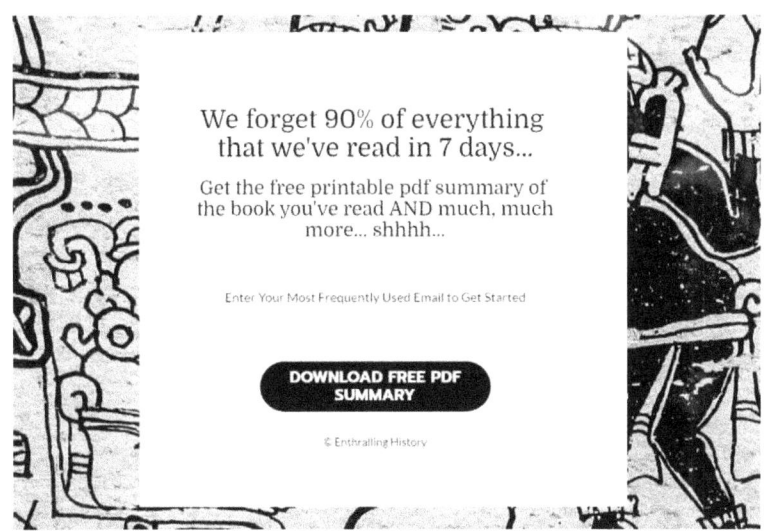

Stop for a moment. We have a free bonus set up for you. The problem is this: we forget 90% of everything that we read after 7 days. Crazy fact, right? Here's the solution: we've created a printable, 1-page pdf summary for this book that you're reading now. All you have to do to get your free pdf summary is to go to the following website: https://livetolearn.lpages.co/enthrallinghistory/

Or, Scan the QR code!

Once you do, it will be intuitive. Enjoy, and thank you!

Table of Contents

INTRODUCTION: GERMANY BEFORE IT WAS GERMANY 1
CHAPTER 1: ANCIENT GERMANIC TRIBES 3
CHAPTER 2: THE RISE OF THE HOLY ROMAN EMPIRE 8
CHAPTER 3: THE RISE OF BARBAROSSA AND THE TEUTONIC KNIGHTS 18
CHAPTER 4: THE REFORMATION AND MARTIN LUTHER 24
CHAPTER 5: THE THIRTY YEARS' WAR AND THE PEACE OF WESTPHALIA 33
CHAPTER 6: THE ENLIGHTENMENT AND THE RISE OF PRUSSIA 40
CHAPTER 7: THE NAPOLEONIC ERA AND THE CONFEDERATION OF THE RHINE 48
CHAPTER 8: REVOLUTION TO UNIFICATION 54
CHAPTER 9: THE WORLD WARS: TURMOIL AND TRANSFORMATION 63
CHAPTER 10: THE POSTWAR AND COLD WAR ERA 76
CHAPTER 11: REUNIFICATION AND BEYOND: MODERN GERMANY 83
CONCLUSION 86
HERE'S ANOTHER BOOK BY ENTHRALLING HISTORY THAT YOU MIGHT LIKE 88
FREE LIMITED TIME BONUS 89
FURTHER READING AND REFERENCE 90
IMAGE SOURCES 91

Introduction: Germany Before It Was Germany

It sounds like a terrible oxymoron to say it, but it needs to be said anyway. Germany is both ancient and relatively new. The history of this unique part of the world can be traced back to the ancient past, but the actual modern-day state of Germany dates back only to 1871. This nation-state is quite young in comparison to many other modern-day nation-states. Even that upstart newcomer, the United States of America, is older than Germany since the US was established in 1776!

However, when we speak of German history, we are considering more than the establishment of the modern-day state of Germany. Before the current boundaries of Germany were established, there were many other incarnations of Germanic statehood.

This historic land rests at an important crossroads, where Western Europe meets Central Europe. Other nations, such as France, Spain, and Great Britain, are clearly defined by geographic boundaries. Many of these boundaries date back for centuries. The boundaries of Germany are not as clearly defined, though, and they are not created so much due to rivers, mountains, and oceans as they are to abstract thinking.

It is a region where countless people groups have moved back and forth during the course of history and have established various coalitions among each other. This regional evolution can actually be traced as far back as the Neanderthals, who were named after Germany's "Neander

Valley," where their skeletal remains were found. The Neanderthals, which are considered to be the hominid cousins of modern humans, made their way into Central Europe after the end of the last Ice Age.

The Neanderthals thrived for quite some time before facing a massive extinction event. No one is sure what exactly happened to the Neanderthals, but it is believed they were deeply affected by the arrival of the *Homo sapiens* (modern humans). Either these early humans killed them or interbred with them; perhaps it was a combination of both. At any rate, the people who followed in their footsteps began to settle down and farm the land. With their food source secure, they began to perfect their language and culture. Since these people groups existed before any historical records, they are categorized by the artifacts that they left behind. The Funnelbeaker culture, for example, named after the prevalent pottery they crafted, is believed to have thrived in the region by 3900 BCE and remained a prevalent presence all the way until 600 BCE.

Prehistoric peoples, such as the Funnelbeakers, would soon be supplanted by a much more sophisticated tribal group known as the Celts. The Celts would come to dominate much of Central and Western Europe, spreading from the mainland all the way to Great Britain. The Celts would eventually butt heads with the growing Mediterranean power of the Romans.

In 390 BCE, Celtic tribes actually raided Rome, which was the capital of what was then the Roman Republic. These Germanic peoples first entered into the historical record due to their encounters with the Romans. As time passed, the growing powerhouse of Rome had to come to grips with the wild Germanic tribes on its frontiers. All oxymorons aside, this confederation of roving warriors was Germany before it was Germany.

Chapter 1: Ancient Germanic Tribes

The notion of a nation-state named Germany taking up space somewhere in Central Europe is so ingrained in the modern consciousness that it can be a bit jarring to realize that Germany, as we know it today, did not exist for much of recorded history. It is true that there have been Germanic peoples, languages, customs, principalities, and even various pseudo-empires for thousands of years. However, the modern-day nation-state of Germany did not actually come about until the 19th century.

As mentioned, Germany's history goes much deeper than that. The first designation of a Germanic region came about because of Julius Caesar. Yes, this would-be dictator of the Roman Republic led his armies into the wilderness of Central Europe, where he encountered fierce Germanic tribes. He ended up calling the region Germania.

After Julius Caesar died and the Roman Republic had transformed itself into the Roman Empire, Roman Emperor Augustus became determined to bring the Germanic tribes north of the empire to heel. He sent troops over the borders of Roman Gaul (France), past the Rhine River, and into Germania itself.

The Romans were initially able to subdue the Germans, but in 9 CE, something unexpected happened. A revolt broke out, and a massive German force surrounded the Roman positions. The Battle of Teutoburg Forest saw an entire legion of Rome's best troops pulverized.

The Romans retreated, and the outposts in Germania were lost. Augustus was so shocked by this outburst that he did not even try to retake this lost ground. It was not until he was succeeded by Emperor Tiberius in 14 CE that further expeditions were sent to try and tame the Germans.

Tiberius was not all that successful, and after several failed attempts, he decided to maintain the Roman borderlands at the Rhine and leave it at that. Just west of the Rhine, the Romans established the provinces of Germania Superior and Germania Inferior.

Perhaps the best-known historical reference about Germania from that time is the work of Roman historian Tacitus, whose work *Germania* sought to describe the region and its people as the Romans understood them at the time. This work, said to have been crafted around 98 CE, described the Germanic tribes as being wild and untamed.

As an indication of their perceived warlike nature, he famously described the Germanic rite of passage for Germanic youths as being the gifting of arms, whereas for Romans, it was the donning of a toga.[1] Both represent articles of importance for both civilizations, with the Roman toga representing intellectual refinement and responsibility and the German sword representing unbridled power.

A Roman bronze figure depicting a Germanic man.[1]

---

[1] Ozment, Steven. *A Mighty Fortress.* 2004. Pg. 22.

Even though Tacitus described the Germans as barbarians, he expressed admiration for their tenacity. He especially admired the fact that the Germans seemed to choose tribal leaders based on their exploits in battle. Leadership was based more on merit than heredity.

Another interesting observation that Tacitus had about these Germanic tribes was what he contended to be their rather transparent nature. Rather than behaving in the cunning Machiavellian mannerisms that the Romans were used to, he described the Germans as holding nothing back as it pertained to their feelings. As Tacitus put it, they "blurted out their innermost thoughts—every soul [laying itself] bare."[i]

One could argue that this trait of candid openness has been passed down, as it is something we can see in German culture today. Many who visit Germany have been struck by the forthright nature of German conversation. And if anyone has ever taken a course in German, they might be forewarned not to take an expression such as "Wie geht es Ihnen?" ("How are you?") lightly. In the English-speaking world, we frequently greet one another with this inquiry, expecting nothing more than a simple reply of "Doing good." But if you were to ask a German, "Wie geht es Ihnen?" you might get an unexpected earful. Ask a random stranger on a German street how they are doing, and they might enter into a diatribe about how they woke up with a terrible headache, were late for work, and were reprimanded by their boss!

The people of Roman Gaul and Roman Germania tended to blend together. Germanic tribes raided one another on each side of the Rhine as much as they intermarried each other. Even though today we have a distinct conception of those who are French and those who are German, this was not the case back then.

Germanic peoples fit into a wide category of tribes in both Germania and Gaul, so there is much confusion as to who should be considered Germanic in the first place. Historians still struggle to figure out whether a revered figure such as Charlemagne should be considered French or German. Most, however, contend that Charlemagne and his Frankish brethren were an amalgamation of the two. They were pseudo-French and pseudo-German since neither nationality existed at the time. The ancestors of these regions prolifically intermingled with one another.

---

[i] Ozment, Steven. *A Mighty Fortress*. 2004. Pg. 22.

This intermingling created the powerhouse known as the Kingdom of the Franks. Again, some see the origin of France in the Franks, while others see Germanic roots. Nevertheless, the Frankish kingdom did stem from Germanic tribes that settled in Central and Western Europe.

The Franks were not the only Germanic tribe in the region at the time. They had plenty of competitors, primarily in the form of the Visigoths, the Ostrogoths, the Lombards, and the Vandals. Of these four groups, the Visigoths proved the most problematic for the Romans.

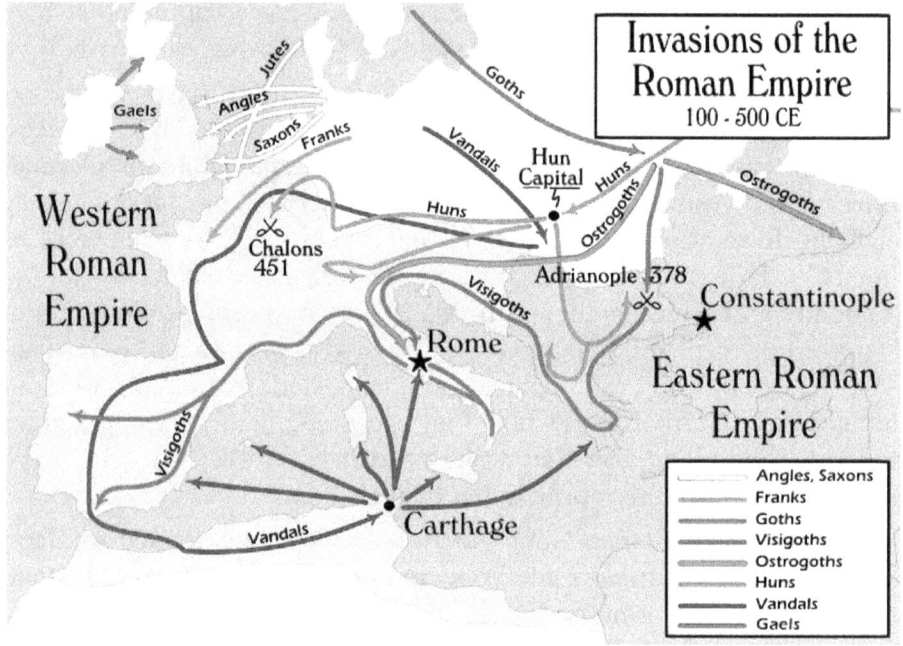

Invasions of the Roman Empire by Germanic tribes.[2]

The Visigoths took part in numerous engagements against the Romans in the late 4th and early 5th centuries CE, culminating in a brazen invasion of Rome itself in 410. This invasion was led by Visigoth chieftain Alaric. Alaric and his warriors sent a tremendous shock through the Roman Empire, as they sacked the city of Rome of all of its valuables, depleting the average Roman of their morale.[i]

However, perhaps even more consequential than the sacking of Rome was the fact that many of the Germanic tribes had become integrated into the Roman military. Toward the end of the Western

---

[i] Benjamin, G. Craig. *The Big History of Civilizations*. 2016. Pg. 184.

Roman Empire, Germanic warriors were increasingly used as auxiliary troops. These Germanic peoples fought alongside the Romans and became quite acquainted with Roman culture.[i]

After the inevitable fall of the Western Roman Empire in the 5th century, a long succession of various Germanic warring tribes led to the rise of the Franks, who were led by their indomitable leader, Clovis. This Germanic warlord was well acquainted with the Romans. He had served with them on various campaigns prior to Rome's collapse. He was influenced by both Roman governance and the Roman Catholic religion.

Clovis is said to have experienced a profound conversion to Christianity, and in what was considered "Germanic custom," his people followed suit. This was how the Franks became Christian. Their descendants would eventually cobble together a Germanic superstate, which included modern-day Germany, France, and northern Italy. This German kingdom, which was breathed into existence in the 9th century, would come to be known as the Holy Roman Empire.

---

[i] Ozment, Steven. *A Mighty Fortress*. 2004. Pg. 25.

Chapter 2: The Rise of the Holy Roman Empire

In 768 CE, Charles the Great, better known as Charlemagne, came into a great inheritance. He was bequeathed an extensive domain that reached from central Germany all the way to the Pyrenees. Charlemagne was a successful ruler and was soon able to expand his domain even farther until his power reached all the way into central Italy.

This brought Charlemagne into close contact with the pope of the Roman Catholic Church, Leo III, who was a virtual head of state over his own dwindling holdings in Rome. Ever since the fall of the Western Roman Empire, the pope had been wheeling and dealing with a multitude of warlords in order to keep his head afloat. There was still an emperor in the Eastern capital of Greek-speaking Constantinople, but the Eastern emperor, who was traditionally held responsible for protecting the pope, could often do very little when push came to shove.

This led the popes to become Machiavellian realists in temperament, siding with whoever was best suited to preserve them and the church. However, Pope Leo III had run afoul of his usual benefactors. He had just succeeded the previous pope, Adrian I, and there were factions that did not approve of his succession. Two of Adrian's nephews, Paschalis and Campulus, in particular, did not approve of the new pope and began to stir up trouble.[i]

---

[i] McCabe, Joseph. *A History of the Popes.* 1939. Pg. 172.

Paschalis and Campulus (just like their uncle Adrian) were from a prominent Roman family and felt entitled to try and influence public discourse as they saw fit. They were dismayed when Leo III was elected as pope, and they wanted to let their discontent be heard. They galvanized others to their cause.

On April 25th, 799, during the religious feast day of St. Mark, some of the most vocal of these dissenters struck.[i] Pope Leo III was leading a religious procession through the streets of Rome. The pope was riding on top of a horse, and the rest of his clergy followed behind. Riding alongside the pope were none other than Paschalis and Campulus.

At first sight, it seemed that the two brothers had temporarily put aside their differences with the pope in order to show solidarity for the religious holiday. But this was not the case. The two had secretly stationed a group of heavily armed men along the procession route, and they were ready to ambush the pope. And sure enough, as soon as the pope approached them, they jumped up from their positions and began their assault.

They knocked the pope right off his horse and then pulled him to the side. They attempted to cut out the pope's tongue and blind him. This was a sign of disgrace back in those days. Someone who had their eyes and tongue removed was typically seen as not only being adequately chastised but also being entirely eliminated as a threat. It would be difficult for leaders (kings, emperors, and even popes) to continue in a leadership role after being blinded. And how could they issue orders without their tongue?

It is not entirely clear what happened next or how extensive Pope Leo III's injuries were in the aftermath. There are legendary stories about this event. They claim that the pope's eyes were indeed cut out but later miraculously reformed in his eye sockets.[ii] Other accounts insist that there were enough papal supporters on hand that day, and they were able to intervene and drive the attackers off before anything too damaging occurred.

At any rate, in the aftermath of this terrible altercation, Pope Leo III turned to the powerful King Charlemagne, who had expanded his reach all the way to his doorstep, for protection. Some of the nobles protested

---

[i] McCabe, Joseph. *A History of the Popes.* 1939. Pg. 173.

[ii] McCabe, Joseph. *A History of the Popes.* 1939. Pg. 173.

this protection and sent an indictment to Charlemagne, which accused the pope of various crimes, including corruption and the general mismanagement of the papacy. Charlemagne sent some of his own nobles to investigate these claims, but they ultimately found no fault with the pope.[i]

Pope Leo III ultimately returned the favor Charlemagne had given him. In acknowledgment of Charlemagne's growing power and the Eastern Roman Empire's shrinking influence, Pope Leo III crowned Charlemagne emperor on Christmas Day, December 25th, 800 CE. Some believe that Pope Leo III did this under duress, but there is no evidence to say one way or the other. It is possible that Pope Leo III did this to strengthen his own position. What would be better for the papacy than to align with the strongest ruler in Europe?

Although it is a complicated narrative to pinpoint exact dates to, some mark this day as the moment that the Holy Roman Empire was born. Other scholars believe the Holy Roman Empire began with Otto I because Charlemagne's empire did not last that long.

This move sent shockwaves throughout the Christian world and would ultimately lead to a schism between the East and the West. The Great Schism would not occur until 1054, but the long process of disentanglement between the Eastern and Western Churches had already begun by 1000 CE. Although the pope really had no choice but to cozy up with the powerful Charlemagne, the Eastern heads of state and church cried heresy, and fractures between the Latin Catholic Church and the Greek Orthodox Church began to emerge.

Interestingly, as much as Charlemagne's crowning was met with disdain by Eastern Christians, he was actually recognized by Eastern Muslims. This footnote in history is overlooked, but it has been said that in this pre-Crusades world, Charlemagne set up embassies in Jerusalem and even Baghdad. He was apparently eager to shore up diplomatic relations with the Islamic powerbrokers of the Middle East.

His efforts were successful to some degree. In October 802 CE, Caliph Harun al-Rashid of the Abbasid dynasty sent Charlemagne a rather extravagant gift to congratulate him on his coronation. Fittingly acknowledging the new "elephant in the room," he sent the new Western Roman emperor (a title disputed by the Eastern Roman

---

[i] McCabe, Joseph. *A History of the Popes*. 1939. Pg. 174.

emperors) an elephant. The caliph also sent extravagant silk robes, exotic spices, expensive perfumes, and even a water clock. However, the elephant, supposedly named Abu al-Abbas, was the most frequently cited gift in the chronicles of the day.

Charlemagne apparently loved his elephant, and he also liked the idea of keeping diplomatic doors open in the Middle East. As much as Christianity and Islam were at odds during this era, Charlemagne was willing to set aside religious differences if he could forge a mutually beneficial alliance. It also cannot be forgotten that both Charlemagne and the caliph had a potential common enemy in the form of the disgruntled Byzantines.

At the time, the Byzantines were ruled by Empress Irene. Considering the disparity between male and female rulers at the time, Empress Irene was not always given the recognition she deserved. The fact that now the pope had turned his back on her in favor of Charlemagne did not help this situation.

The Byzantine empress was not happy with Charlemagne's claim as emperor, but even if she were able to raise a sufficient army to challenge the forces of Charlemagne in battle, she had to worry about the caliph allying with Charlamagne. That would open up a second front right in the Byzantine ruler's backyard.

There was also another, perhaps even more practical, reason for Charlemagne to align himself with Caliph Harun al-Rashid and the Abbasid dynasty. The Abbasids had toppled and supplanted a previous Islamic dynasty, the Umayyads. The Umayyads were driven out of Baghdad but had set up their new base in Córdoba, Spain, which was still under Islamic rule at the time of Charlemagne's coronation.

The Umayyads presented a real threat to Charlemagne's southern borders. By having an alliance with the Abbasids, Charlemagne gave himself considerable breathing room. Neither the Umayyads nor the Byzantines were ready to stoke the wrath of the powerful Abbasids and Franks.

All of this goes to show that Charlemagne the Great was not just a powerful warrior king. He was also a pragmatic political broker. He knew the realpolitik of the day and sought to use it to the best of his advantage.

Charlemagne was a benevolent patron of the pope and the Catholic Church. He left the pope in control of Rome and even gifted him more territory while maintaining control of much of northern Italy, France, and Germany.

Empress Irene was deposed in 802 and was succeeded by Emperor Nikephoros I. The East and the West would then come together briefly when the Byzantine emperor agreed to the Treaty of Aachen, which acknowledged Charlemagne as the emperor of the West as long as Charlemagne promised to stay away from Mediterranean territory that the Byzantines had been desperately attempting to cling to, such as the important port city of Venice.

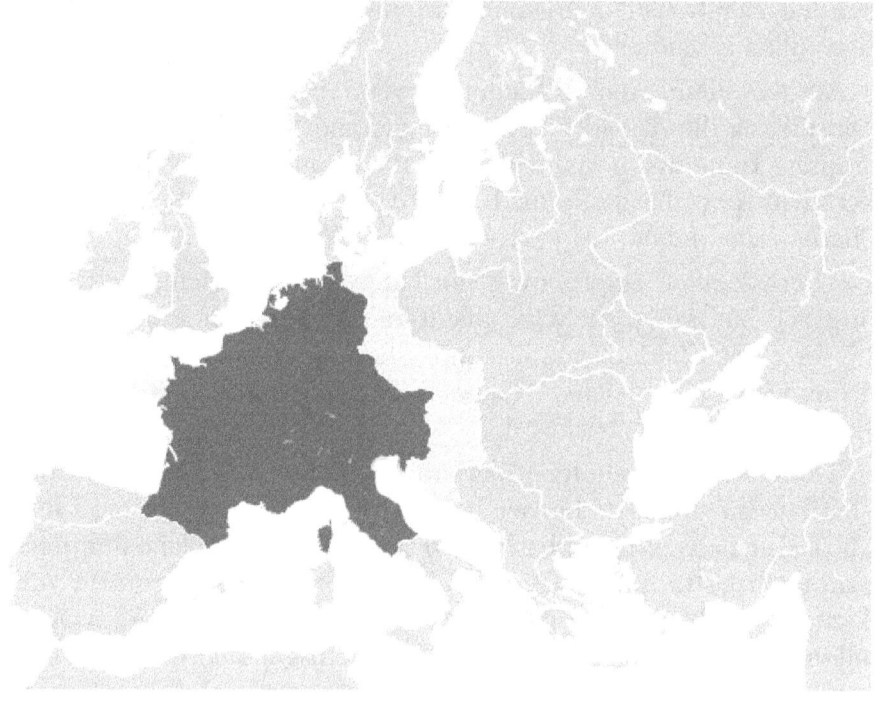

The Carolingian Empire in 814 CE.[3]

Charlemagne ultimately died in 814 CE and ceded his realm to his son, Louis the Pious. Louis found governing the large empire difficult and decided to divide the territory between his three sons: Louis, Lothair, and Charles the Bald.

No sooner than this new system was devised, the three successors began to squabble over it. Arguments over just who would get what led to armed conflict. The matter was finally resolved in 843 CE by way of the Treaty of Verdun.

This treaty handed over the region of West Francia, which basically made up the modern borders of France, to Charles the Bald. The region known as East Francia, which roughly consisted of what we now know as Germany, went to Louis. Lothair got the short end of the stick, as he was given an exceedingly narrow strip of land locked directly between West and East Francia. It was dubbed Lotharingia.

Lotharingia was narrow, but it was long, reaching from northern Italy all the way up to the Netherlands. It was also entirely indefensible. Poor Lothair must have known that he faced armed aggression from both of his brothers on either side of his domain if he angered them.

East Francia roughly constituted the boundaries of modern-day Germany and was made up of the German duchies of Franconia, Saxony, Swabia, and Bavaria. These lands would later be tied together in a confederation under King Henry the Fowler in 919 until the end of his long reign in 936. As one may guess, this king was an avid hunter and was dedicated to the fine art of falconry. The term "Regnum Teutonicorum" came to designate the lands of King Henry. The term can be roughly translated as "Kingdom of the Germans."

Henry managed to incorporate Lorraine back into the German kingdom, seizing this thoroughly French territory in 925 CE. He also took control of Bohemia and pushed into Saxony. He invaded Denmark toward the end of his reign, thereby making the region of Schleswig part of his dominion as well. Henry put several fortifications in place along the frontiers of the kingdom and kept a wary eye on the Magyars, who were saber rattling to the east.

Upon Henry's death in 936, Otto I was made king by the archbishop of Mainz and Cologne at the city of Aachen. He truly had his work cut out for him. One of his greatest accomplishments was securing the Bavarian Eastern March, which had been under threat for some time by the encroaching Hungarian Magyars. Otto defeated the Magyars, and the Bavarian Eastern March would go on to become German-speaking Austria.

Otto also managed to push traditional Germany's eastern border all the way to the Oder River. This is the current eastern boundary of Germany today. Otto then threw his weight around in Italy and managed to gain authority over who could become an abbot or a bishop.

This powerful clout in the Catholic Church came with the supposed responsibility of the German king being the protector of the Roman

Church and the pope. Otto was officially recognized as the Holy Roman emperor of the German nation. It is a confusing term, and it would later inspire the derision of great satirists, such as Voltaire, who once remarked that the Holy Roman Empire was neither holy nor Roman nor even a true empire. However, it was a term that would remain in force for quite a long time.

The Holy Roman Empire between 972 and 1032 CE.[4]

The empire certainly was not without its problems. The emperor being in charge of the appointments of bishops and abbots was a source of major disagreements. The first real crisis between the Catholic church and the German state took place during Henry III's reign. Henry reigned from 1046 to 1056, and during this period, the Catholic Church found itself in a transitional moment. Henry III had to deal with a papal crisis, which left the Roman Catholic Church without an effective leader on the papal throne. At one point, three different popes claimed to be the pontiff—Benedict IX, Sylvester III, and Gregory VI. Henry III settled the matter by deposing all of them before appointing Suidger of Bamberg, otherwise known as Clement II, as the next pope. Although the pope had crowned the first Holy Roman emperor, Charlemagne, in the year 800, Henry III started a new tradition of having the Holy Roman emperor essentially become a papal kingmaker.

During the last couple of years of Henry III's reign, the fractures between the Western and Eastern Churches finally came to a head, resulting in the Great Schism in 1054. The Great Schism happened because of differences in the ritualistic practices of the two churches and the notion of where the ultimate earthly authority should be placed. The pope believed he was the supreme ruler, while the patriarch believed differently. The Eastern Church had long criticized the Western Church's seeming subordinance to Western rulers, such as Henry III, and decided to cut ties for good.

After Henry III's death in 1056, the papacy sought to reform the system so that the Catholic Church would have more say over who would become pope than the state. This discord came to a head in 1078 with the Investiture Controversy, which was launched under Pope Gregory VII. This set Pope Gregory VII at odds with Holy Roman Emperor Henry IV. Henry was just fine with the system of bishopric and abbot appointments and was deeply dismayed that this pope wanted to interfere with the status quo.

Henry even went as far as to try and annul Gregory's status as pope. He began to refer to him as "Hildebrand." This was Pope Gregory VII's original name prior to him becoming pontiff in 1073. Henry was trying to assert that Gregory should have never become pope in the first place and that his current status was invalid.

Gregory's rise to the position of pope was not without its controversy. Henry seized upon the discontent with his election and used it to criticize him. He also convened a group of German bishops who were under his sway and had them sign a letter that officially condemned and castigated the pope. The letter was filled with all kinds of anti-pope propaganda and innuendo, accusing Pope Gregory of a multitude of infractions. At one point, it even insinuated that Gregory was having an improper relationship with one of his parishioners. Copies of the letter were made, and they were circulated all throughout the Holy Roman Empire. It was designed to be as scandalous and incendiary as possible, but Pope Gregory refused to back down. In fact, he took the drastic step of excommunicating Henry.

Henry was seen as a heretic at odds with the Roman Catholic Church. This was not an easy thing for Henry to face at the time, and it meant that many of those who were supposed to be under his charge began to actively question his own authority to reign. In essence, both the pope and the Holy Roman emperor were insisting that neither one of them was legitimate or fit enough to lead.

The two heads of the Western medieval world had become completely at odds with each other. Henry IV, however, underestimated the support that the pope had from German nobles and was ultimately forced to beg the pope for forgiveness. Henry IV is said to have stood barefoot in the snow outside of the Castle of Canossa in the Alps, where the pope had taken refuge. Henry asked the pope to rescind his excommunication.

Pope Gregory realized that it was in his best interest to do so, and he finally relented and did just that. In this round of battles between the Catholic Church and the Holy Roman Empire, the pope was clearly victorious, as were the various German princes who supported the pope instead of Henry IV. From this point forward, the German princes and, later, the German electors would be crucial for the Holy Roman emperor's election and ability to maintain power.

Yes, the Catholic Church had won this round, but this was not the end of the story. As soon as the pope took back his excommunication of Henry IV, a civil war ensued between Henry and a substantial portion of the German princes who did not back him. It seems that even though the pope was willing to grant clemency to Henry IV, not all of the powerful German princes were as willing to do so. These wily opportunists believed once a heretic, always a heretic, and they preferred to ignore the absolution that the pope had rendered. Henry IV, who was scorned by his peers, would ultimately die in 1106. He was unable to regain the footing he once held.

Henry perished with half his realm still up in arms against him, including his own son, Henry V. Ultimately, Henry V's bid to side with the pope and his father's rivals cost him his own power during his reign. Henry V had to deal with the Concordat of Worms, which had him give up almost all of his control of the influential bishoprics in northern Italy.

A considerable amount of power had shifted from the office of the Holy Roman emperor to the pope and the German prince-electors, whose prestige had increased. The Holy Roman Empire had essentially developed into what can only be termed an electoral monarchy. Just like the president of the United States is elected by an electoral college scattered over all fifty states, the Holy Roman emperor would be elected by special electors from all across the Holy Roman Empire. Such a comparison is very general, of course, but the similarities provide a decent example.

The electors developed the notion that the emperor was primus inter pares, or "first among equals." The Holy Roman emperor was not really any greater than the electors; he was simply the one who was chosen to be in charge. This concept would be important, not just during the election of emperors but also during their reign. Powerful electors would hold much clout and would often weigh in on important matters of state.

Martin Luther, for example, famously rocked the Catholic Church with his calls for reformation, yet it was an elector who ended up holding the balance of power. Even though both the pope and the sitting Holy Roman emperor wanted to punish the rebellious monk, he was actively protected by a powerful German elector. This elector managed to thwart any direct action being taken against Luther.

It did not stop Luther from being condemned and excommunicated. It also did not stop the Holy Roman emperor from declaring Luther an outlaw and basically suggesting that if any random citizen of the realm were to dispatch with Luther, they would not be punished. However, it did stop any direct official action from being taken by either the Catholic Church or the Holy Roman Empire.

We will discuss these happenings in greater depth in the next chapter, but for now, it is important to know that this weakening of executive power helped to make such things as Luther's Reformation possible in the first place.

Chapter 3: The Rise of Barbarossa and the Teutonic Knights

After Henry V perished on May 23rd, 1125, he was succeeded by Lothair III, who was elected by a group of imperial prince-electors. He was already in his fifties at the time, so it was generally accepted that his reign would be brief. He reigned until his death in 1137 at the age of sixty-two. Stepping into the void was Conrad III. Conrad was just an interim ruler. His nephew, Frederick Barbarossa, was designated as his heir apparent.

Frederick was a force to be reckoned with. An intellectual and a warrior, he reigned as king of the Germans from 1152 to 1155. In the fateful year of 1155, he was made Holy Roman emperor. Frederick often found himself at odds with many of the German

A golden bust of Frederick Barbarossa.[5]

princes, just as many of his predecessors had. In order to offset these difficulties, Frederick sought to gain greater support in Italy. He cozied up to power brokers in Italy's powerful northern cities. He also became a favorite of Pope Adrian IV by putting down an insurrection in Rome.

Frederick would become the most known for his crusading efforts. Although the Germans were latecomers to the Crusades, Frederick would become an enthusiastic Crusader during a pivotal phase of the conflict. During Frederick's reign, Jerusalem fell to Islamic warlord Saladin in 1188.

The First Crusade, which was called in 1095, had seen the successful capture of Jerusalem by Crusader forces, and just short of a century later, the Crusaders' grip on Jerusalem had slipped. Holy Roman Emperor Frederick was determined to lead the charge to take it back. He hooked up with French King Philip Augustus (Philip II) and the leading light of England, Richard the Lionheart, and set out for what would become known as the King's Crusade, which was, in reality, the third major official Crusade to the Middle East.

Initially, Barbarossa and his countrymen seemed poised to make a real difference in the conflict, but after Barbarossa perished in a freak accident, all hell broke loose. Frederick Barbarossa had tried to cross a river on horseback but had underestimated the force of the water that flowed through it. Stories differ, but most say he drowned in the water due to his heavy armor.

It was clear to most that he had drowned, even though a legend would develop insisting that Frederick did not die but instead somehow entered into a state of suspended animation. The most popular of these myths suggests that he was slumbering under Mount Kyffhäuser in Thuringia. It may seem a bit unusual, but such myths were fairly common. In this tale, one can even see echoes of the British story of King Arthur. In both legends, it is suggested that the slumbering monarchs are simply waiting for the day their countrymen might need them most. At any rate, as of this writing, no one has heard from Frederick or King Arthur.

Frederick's death threw the Holy Roman Empire into chaos. It was indeed a chaotic period, but something very notable in German history occurred. Around this time, an order of German knights was established.

Previously, the Knights Templar and the Knights Hospitaller had been the ones to carry out heroic deeds in the Holy Land. Around the year 1190, the order of German crusaders known as the Teutonic Knights was established. The Teutonic Knights made their base in the coastal city of Acre in the Levant and took part in the Third Crusade, which sought to recover Jerusalem.

The Teutonic Knights began in a similar fashion as the Hospitallers. The Hospitallers were known for establishing special hospitals to take care of the wounded. The Teutonic Knights began by establishing the Order of the Hospital of St. Mary. In the aftermath of the fall of Jerusalem, which saw refugees flood into Acre, such field hospitals were crucial.

Once the Order of the Hospital of St. Mary began to move beyond just tending the wounded to take part in military operations, they shifted from being just caregivers to being a branch of warriors in their own right. They also found a lucrative side gig by keeping watch on the port city of Acre, collecting tolls from those who passed through.

The situation in Acre would soon become untenable. As Islamic armies began to drive the Christian Crusaders into the sea, the Teutonic Knights would eventually have to move their base of operations out of the Levant. In 1210, under the leadership of Teutonic Grand Master Hermann von Salza, the knights relocated to Transylvania. This was done at the request of the king of Hungary. At that time, Transylvania was on the fringes of Christian Europe, with various factions warring against each other. It was also on the front lines of the ongoing struggle between the forces of Islam and Christianity since Transylvania was in the path of the rising Muslim power, the Ottoman Turks, who were pushing out of Asia Minor (modern-day Turkey) into the Balkans of southeastern Europe.

In return for their efforts in this dangerous region, the king of Hungary pledged to give the Teutonic Knights special perks and privileges, such as tax-exempt land. This allowed the Teutonic Knights to take over large tracts of land in the wild border regions of Hungary and Transylvania. They brought German settlers with them who would not have to bother forking over money to the king.

The situation initially worked well enough, but by 1225, the Hungarians became wary of this growing German enclave and forced the Teutonic Knights and their followers to relocate once again. This change of plans, facilitated by official papal marching orders, led the knights to take part in the Prussian Crusade. The region known as Prussia no longer exists, but during the time of the Teutonic Knights, it was a vast swathe of relatively untamed land along the Baltic coasts of northeastern Europe.

With the backing of the pope and Poland's Duke Konrad I of Masovia, the Teutonic Knights launched their own personal holy war against the pagan residents of the region. The Teutonic Knights would prove to be highly successful in forcibly converting the locals and wresting lands away from them.

It seems the establishment of permanent castles by the Teutonic Knights broke the Prussians' backs. Prior to this, both Polish and German nobles launched attacks on the pagan Prussians. The warfare was usually effective at first, but after initially driving the Prussians back, they would regroup and overwhelm the Polish and German intruders. It was only once formidable forts were established up and down the Vistula River that the Teutonic Knights were able to effectively stand their ground.

Their fortresses were formidable, and the knights were highly skilled at defending them, even from a multitude of Prussians. The Vistula River provided an obvious source of easy transport since waterways such as these were basically the superhighways of the medieval world.

This strategic initiative finally put a dent in the Prussian armor, and the Teutonic Knights and the Germans who settled around their fortresses would continue to expand their reach into the Prussian frontiers.

In the meantime, the Holy Roman Empire had gained a dynamic new ruler in the form of Frederick II. Frederick reigned from 1225 until his death in 1250. He left a lasting impression not just on his realm but also on all of world history. Frederick II ruled through a combination of martial might, diplomacy, and outright bribery. The bribes were mostly needed to hold back rebellious German princes in his own backyard, while martial might and a surprising degree of diplomacy were used during his efforts during the Crusades.

Holy Roman Emperor Frederick II.[6]

Frederick II famously negotiated an agreement with the Muslim powers of the Middle East to allow Christians to temporarily have control of Jerusalem so long as a kind of sharing agreement was arranged with the locals. This level of diplomatic cooperation was relatively unheard of at the time, and the arrangement, as unique as it was, was generally despised by both local Muslims and local Christians.

Frederick II was known as a cultured and skilled statesman. Even so, conflicts in Italy, where Frederick sought to exert his authority, would lead to a falling out with the pope. Due to these difficulties, Frederick II was excommunicated on more than one occasion.

Despite the success of the Teutonic Knights and Frederick II's impressive feats of diplomacy, following Frederick II's demise in 1250, the Holy Roman Empire had lost considerable clout on the international scene. The century that followed would see the power and prestige of the Holy Roman Empire continue to wane until it constituted little more than a very loose confederation of oligarchs under a very weak figurehead.

As noted, Frederick II had been excommunicated on multiple occasions, which had allowed a conglomeration of unruly German princes to reign over their own autonomous regions. The Holy Roman Empire had been weakened and fractured, and the other great powers of Europe were content to keep it that way. It was much better for them to have a weak and divided Holy Roman Empire than to have a powerful nation on their doorsteps.

However, their actions unwittingly provided the perfect breeding ground for the Reformation. Due to the decentralized and autonomous regions of the German realm, Martin Luther was allowed to rail against the pope and find refuge among German prince-electors who were willing to shelter him.

Chapter 4: The Reformation and Martin Luther

"I hoped the pope would protect me, for I had so fortified my theses with proofs from the Bible and papal decretals that I was sure he would condemn Tetzel and bless me. But when I expected a benediction from Rome, there came thunder and lightning instead, and I was treated like the sheep who had roiled the wolf's water. Tetzel went scot-free, and I must submit to be devoured."

-Martin Luther[i]

It can be said that by the time of the 14th century, the Holy Roman Empire, as well as the world, was going through quite a bit of change. As it pertains to the Holy Roman Empire, a major event occurred in 1356. An imperial decree called the Golden Bull was issued by Holy Roman Emperor Charles IV. According to this decree, succession to the throne would be overseen by seven prince-electors. These seven important prince-electors of the German confederation would wield the power as it pertained to who would be elected as the next Holy Roman emperor. This decree would remain in effect without much change until the Thirty Years' War in 1648.

In between all of this, something else eventful happened: the Reformation of the Catholic Church. By this point, the Holy Roman

---

[i] McGiffert, Cushman. *Martin Luther: The Man and His Work.* 1911. Pg. 101.

Empire had become a highly decentralized group of cities, regions, and princes. Unlike the rigid conformity held in much of the rest of Europe, differences of opinion were allowed. However, under the right circumstances, they could easily flourish.

Today, we can admire such rugged individualism, but in the past, this state of affairs was often likened to anarchy. In 1495, Holy Roman Emperor Maximilian I was inspired to establish the so-called "Eternal Peace." This decree was made at an official proceeding of the Holy Roman Empire's deliberating body known as the Diet of Worms. The Diet of Worms was basically a council that took place in the city of the same name. This council did not seek unification exactly; rather, it focused on compromise and cooperation between the different factions of the realm that were so often at odds with each other.

This was an act of near desperation on Maximilian's part. He wanted to bring some order to a realm that was slipping out of the emperor's grip. Some important changes to the civil structure were achieved, such as the creation of an imperial tribunal where grievances could be aired. This was certainly an improvement to the ad hoc system of crime, punishment, and deliberation that previously existed. For a brief moment, the decree seemed to promise some sense of unity in the realm.

However, Maxmillian would perish in 1519, and he had barely accomplished this task. In fact, the realm was more turbulent than ever, as the electors of the Holy Roman Empire vigorously debated who they would elect to the position of Holy Roman emperor. The electors ultimately settled upon Maximillian's grandson Charles V. However, they did so with a series of stipulations.

In exchange for the electors' support, they had Charles agree not to utilize any of the empire's resources for dynastic purposes. He also had to pledge not to bring any foreign troops on German soil. Perhaps most important as it pertains to the coming Reformation was the fact that Charles also pledged not to embark upon any important matters of imperial policy without first consulting with appropriate German counsels, also known as diets.

This agreement would see Martin Luther, who was branded a heretic by the Catholic Church, appear before the Diet or Council of Worms to plead his case. If Charles had not made such agreements and was not so dependent upon the support of the seven electors, Martin Luther could have simply been dragged off to Rome and thrown behind bars.

Before we get too far ahead of ourselves, let us first give a basic summary of how the Reformation itself emerged. The Reformation began on the evening of October 31st, 1517. On this day, a little-known German monk by the name of Martin Luther posted a series of complaints, critiques, and philosophical musings to the doors of Wittenberg Church. This series of notes posted to the church doors would become known as the *Ninety-five Theses*.

Contrary to what you may think, Luther did not choose October 31st because it was Halloween. He actually chose October 31st because it was the day before All Saints' Day, sometimes also known as All Hallows' Day, which takes place on November 1st. He knew that celebrations would begin on All Saints' Day, and multitudes of people would be going in and out of the church's doors. Luther wanted his theses to be the first things these people saw. And they definitely saw them.

It was exceedingly rare for anyone to criticize church doctrine, so the arguments nailed to Wittenberg's doors came as a surprise. Luther's thoughts sparked a dialogue that spread like wildfire.

He had many criticisms of the church, but he strongly disagreed with the pope and his subordinates collecting indulgences. These were offerings of money to clergy with the express promise that the clergy would pray for the deceased in order to lessen their time in purgatory.

One can get into a lengthy debate about the existence of purgatory itself. Many Protestants eventually stopped believing in it altogether. If you were to speak with non-Catholic Christians today, they might be of the opinion that the Catholic Church made the whole thing up. This, however, is not the case.

Purgatory (whether you believe in it or not) was a belief derived from scripture. The notion of purgatory comes from a very specific interpretation of the scripture and is no more "made up" than the belief in the rapture. Now one might disagree with the interpretation of the scripture, but the idea of purgatory is not something that some Catholic priest just arbitrarily made up.

The notion that one could take alms for the dead and pray to save their soul was validated through the scripture as well. Catholics point to a verse in the Book of Maccabees. The Book of Maccabees is considered by most Protestant churches today as part of the Apocrypha (a collection of biblical books that are considered not to be part of canon scripture), but it is still important to both Christianity and Judaism. The Book of Maccabees contains the story of Hannukah.

Maccabees was written during a troubling time in Jewish history when outside powers were trying to dominate the land. After soldiers fighting in one of these many struggles perished, prayers for the deceased were called. Judas Maccabeus took alms for the dead and, assuming their souls to be trapped in an in-between state (like purgatory), prayed for their release.

As we are told in 2nd Maccabees 42-45:

"The noble Judas called on the people to keep themselves free from sin, for they had seen with their own eyes what had happened to the fallen because of their sin. He levied a contribution from each man and sent the total of two thousand silver drachmas to Jerusalem for a sin offering—a fit and proper act in which he took due account of the resurrection. For if he had not been expecting the fallen to rise again, it would have been foolish and superfluous to pray for the dead. But since he had in view the wonderful reward reserved for those who die a godly death, his purpose was a holy and pious one. And this was why he offered an atoning sacrifice to free the dead from the sin."[i]

Of course, one could argue that this was a weak interpretation of the scripture. Fair enough. Martin also dared to challenge it. He even criticized the authority of the pope himself.

Catholics believe that the pope has been imbued with power from on high because of Christ's words to Peter, whom Catholics consider to have been the first pope. Jesus told Peter (whose name actually means rock) that he was the rock on which he would build the church and that the gates of hell would not prevail against it.

Jesus further told Peter that he was going to give him the keys to the kingdom. Peter was told that whatever he bound on Earth would be bound in heaven and that whatever he loosed on Earth would be loosed in heaven. Peter went on to establish the first church in Rome before he was executed by the pagan-believing Romans. This is why he was considered the first pope.

All subsequent popes were believed to have inherited Peter's keys to the kingdom and to have been imbued with the same binding and

---

[i] *The New English Bible with the Apocrypha.* 1970.

loosing power. It was for this reason that a pope and his subordinates felt they could claim they had the power to bind (by way of excommunication) or loosen (by way of lessening one's time in purgatory).

The basic reaction against Martin Luther by the Catholic Church was, "Who the heck is this guy?" and "Who does he think he is to question the already established interpretation of scripture?" The learned clergy of the church just could not believe that someone like Luther would think he knew more than thousands of years of Catholic theologians and that he would dare to spread his interpretation of the Bible.

Even more importantly, the officials in the Catholic Church wanted to stop Luther before his new-fangled ideas infected the masses. In 1520, a papal bull was issued that declared Luther's views were akin to poison. The church really did not want Luther's views to spread too far. Containing Luther's thoughts was deemed all the more imperative in light of the invention of the printing press.

The printing press had been around before 1440 outside of Europe, but it was vastly improved by a German inventor named Johannes Gutenberg. The printing press now used a mobile, metal type instead of wood blocks. The Gutenberg press allowed for information to spread so much faster than old-fashioned handwritten letters ever could.

However, the pope and the Holy Roman emperor had a problem. Wittenberg was the capital of the Electorate of Saxony. The elector of Saxony was crucial to Holy Roman Emperor Charles V's continued success.

The elector of Saxony, Frederick the Wise, ended up throwing in his lot with Martin Luther. Thanks to the support of Frederick the Wise, Luther could continue his revolt against the church without being burned at the stake for heresy.

Frederick did not entirely subscribe to Luther's views. His primary motivation was to ward off outside intervention against a notable, well-known, and increasingly popular local scholar. Frederick was also a huge benefactor of Wittenberg University, where Martin Luther taught. Frederick had actually founded it, and he was not about to let one of his scholars be yanked around. Since Luther had the protection of the elector of Saxony, he was able to send his words off to the printers, allowing for the wider dissemination of his ideas throughout the realm.

Things came to a head when Luther was excommunicated on January 3rd, 1521. Despite this blow, the Catholic Church wanted to give Luther a chance to recant his beliefs. He was called to give an account for himself and present his ideas to the Diet of Worms in 1521. However, Luther failed to convince his detractors, and the label of heretic would remain firmly in place.

Martin Luther making his case in front of the Diet of Worms.[7]

The Holy Roman emperor, who was in attendance, although did not take direct action, declared that Luther was an outlaw. This declaration basically rescinded all of Luther's rights as a citizen and allowed (practically even encouraged) anyone who felt compelled to apprehend him. This meant that any random citizen could kill Luther and would not be held accountable for their actions.

So, even though Luther was not being dragged away in chains by the Holy Roman emperor's entourage, the world had become very dangerous for this Protestant reformer. And as dangerous as it was for Luther, it was very dangerous for others too. Soon, many parts of Germany would be engaged in open warfare between the factions that supported Luther and those who did not. Luther finally made his way back to Wittenberg in 1522 and attempted to somehow get on top of the events that were spiraling out of control. He found that some of his previous supporters were making matters worse for him by stoking fires of revolt and even spreading views that were not his own. For instance, Andreas Karlstadt began to declare infant baptism as a false belief.

There are many Christians today who may speak of one needing to reach the age of accountability in order to be even considered a sinner. This is the notion that one may be too innocent to even know what sin is. However, Saint Augustine, who lived from 354 to 430 CE, trashed this concept a long time ago. He argued that babies were born sinners.

It sounds almost ridiculous, but Augustine actually made a good point. He argued that since a baby is born crying, it is a clear indication of their self-centered, sinning nature at work. Babies are not crying to help others or be of service; they are crying because they want something. They want food, water, warmth, or attention. According to Augustine, this is clearly the selfish, sinful nature of humanity at work. Martin Luther agreed with Augustine's take and found infant baptism quite necessary.

However, Martin Luther had opened up a Protestant Pandora's box, and zealous reformers such as Karlstadt were taking things much further than Luther had intended to take them. At one point, Karlstadt even declared that Martin Luther was a greater stumbling block to reform than the pope. This was a decidedly bizarre conclusion to reach, considering that Martin Luther was the one who had kicked off the Reformation in the first place.

Feelings of disenchantment with Luther among Protestants were seconded by another early Reformation leader, Thomas Müntzer. Thomas Müntzer felt that Luther did not go far enough and called him out for his relatively cozy relationship with the German nobility.

Martin Luther was indeed quite cozy with members of the elite, most especially the elector of Saxony since his protection was vital to his very existence. Reformers such as Müntzer brought up this fact to ridicule Luther as being too soft. Müntzer even railed against Luther by likening him to a "fattened swine."

Luther was just as disenchanted with the Protestant factions. He castigated overly zealous reformers such as Karlstadt and Müntzer as "rioting murderous spirits."

Luther's fears of riots erupted in earnest in 1525 when radical reformers kicked off what became known as the German Peasants' War. This uprising was largely composed of the poorer classes of German society, who had been goaded and convinced by religious radicals like Müntzer to take up arms against the upper class in an attempt to change the status quo—religious, social, and otherwise.

Martin Luther came out strongly against this disturbance. In fact, Luther wrote a fiery tract entitled *Against the Murderous, Thieving Hordes of Peasants*. The title should be pretty clear about what is talked about in this piece.

Luther stated that the peasants who killed and robbed the rich and landed estates while claiming to be doing so in the name of God were the worst kind of blasphemers. He further insisted that the rich nobles had every right to crush the revolt since they were the true wielders of authority. They were merely putting down an uncouth, sinful insurrection of the ugliest kind.

Luther went on the record to state, "Our peasants, however, want to make the goods of other men common, and keep their own for themselves. Fine Christians they are! I think there is not a devil left in hell; they have all gone into the peasants.."[i]

The German authorities eventually crushed the revolt, and Thomas Müntzer was rounded up and killed. The Protestants were certainly in disarray at this point, and it was for this reason that the monk who started it all—Martin Luther—felt compelled to bring some sort of clarity to the madness. He tried his best in 1530 to once again restore some stability by consolidating the views of his theological doctrine with his Augsburg Confession.

This confession of faith expressed Martin's belief in the nature of God, the nature of original sin, and, most importantly, his notion of justification by faith. Luther used biblical references to support his views, especially justification by faith, as he did not wish to follow edicts from the pope requiring penitential works.

Although supported in some sense through the writings of the Apostle Paul, Luther runs into a seeming contradiction since James, in the Book of James, clearly states, "Faith without works is dead." Martin Luther steadfastly disagreed, so much so that he even suggested taking the Book of James out of the Bible and insisted that it was faith and not works that justified the believer.

Martin Luther died in 1546. The turmoil of the Protestant Reformation still very much affected Central Europe. The very year of Luther's death, Holy Roman Emperor Charles V, with renewed

---

[i] McGiffert, Cushman. *Martin Luther: The Man and His Work.* 1911. Pg. 256.

determination to stamp out the Protestants once and for all, sent troops to take on the Protestant stronghold of Saxony.

No longer living in fear of losing the elector of Saxony, Charles captured and imprisoned the elector of the realm, John Frederick I. He then installed his own handpicked elector, Maurice von Wettin.

However, if Charles V thought he could tamper with the "electoral college" of the Holy Roman Empire and tilt the game in his favor by inserting his own elector, he was mistaken. No sooner than Maurice was made elector of Saxony, he turned against the Holy Roman emperor. He allied himself with the other Protestant princes, as well as with France, leading to the outbreak of what became known as the Princes' Revolt in the year 1552.

The outbreak of the Princes' Revolt proved that force would not solve the problems in his realm. Realizing as much, a few years later, in 1555, he convened the nobility at the Diet of Augsburg and issued the Peace of Augsburg, which stipulated that the princes of the various cities in the German realm could basically choose for themselves whether they wished to remain Catholic or Protestant.

Tired and defeated, Charles V died a short time later. The Peace of Augsburg, with its grand concessions that allowed more free will among the princes, was a bandage at best. Even so, it would remain in place for some sixty years before this wound was torn wide open once again in what would become known as the Thirty Years' War.

Chapter 5: The Thirty Years' War and the Peace of Westphalia

In 1618, a violent conflict erupted. This would signal the start of the Thirty Years' War. The origin of this conflict lay in the Holy Roman Empire's desire to maintain control over the electoral state of Bohemia, which was under the influence of the Habsburg dynasty. The Habsburgs, who ruled Austria from 1282 to 1918, first came to prominence in the year 1273. During that fateful year, German prince-electors elected Rudolf of Habsburg as king of the Romans (sometimes also interchangeably called king of the Germans). Being designated as king of the Romans placed Rudolf just a stepping stone away from being hailed as the next Holy Roman emperor.[i]

---

[i] Murray, V. *The Crusades: An Encyclopedia.* 2006. Pg. 1063.

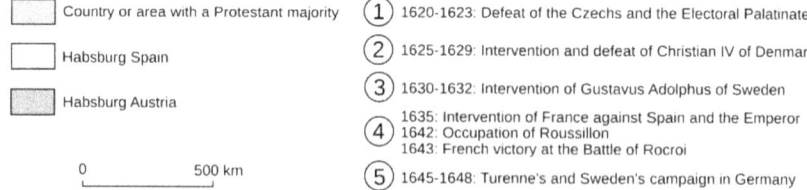

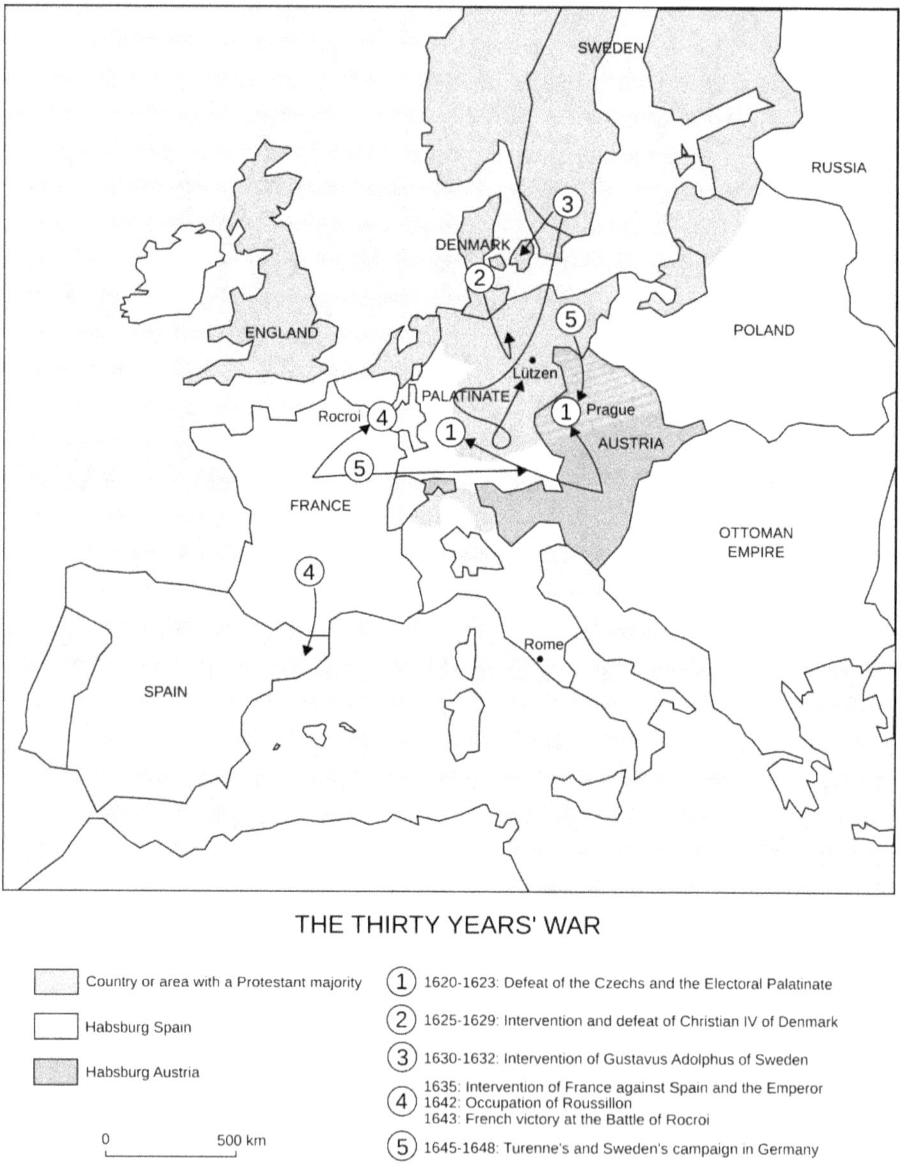
SWEDEN
RUSSIA
DENMARK
ENGLAND
POLAND
Lützen
PALATINATE
Rocroi
Prague
AUSTRIA
FRANCE
OTTOMAN
EMPIRE
Rome
SPAIN
THE THIRTY YEARS' WAR
Country or area with a Protestant majority
Habsburg Spain
Habsburg Austria
0 500 km
1 1620-1623: Defeat of the Czechs and the Electoral Palatinate
2 1625-1629: Intervention and defeat of Christian IV of Denmark
3 1630-1632: Intervention of Gustavus Adolphus of Sweden
4 1635: Intervention of France against Spain and the Emperor
1642: Occupation of Roussillon
1643: French victory at the Battle of Rocroi
5 1645-1648: Turenne's and Sweden's campaign in Germany

Map of the Thirty Years' War.[8]

The trouble began with the rise of Ferdinand II, who reigned from 1619 to 1637, to the throne of the Holy Roman Empire. Ferdinand II was not satisfied with the results of the 1555 Peace of Augsburg. Upon rising to prominence, he sought to roll back the clock, take away previous religious freedoms, and enforce Catholic doctrine. Even though the Peace of Augsburg allowed German princes to determine whether their realms would adhere to Catholicism or Protestantism, Ferdinand II was hell-bent on making everyone in the empire once again become obedient to the Catholic faith.

Just about as soon as it was learned that these changes to the status quo were underway, Protestant leaders began to make their displeasure known. In the Bohemian lands that now make up part of Austria and the modern-day Czech Republic, the reaction was immediate and deadly. The noble lords of the realm decided to shoot (or at least toss) the emperor's messengers. They hurled these diplomats from the window of Prague Castle. Amazingly, the dignitaries reportedly survived since they landed on a large pile of dung in the castle's moat.

Holy Roman Emperor Ferdinand II was none too pleased when he heard of what had happened. This incident marked the beginning of an insurrection in Bohemia, which spread to other Protestant strongholds across the realm. The Holy Roman emperor was not going to take this insurrection lightly and marshaled the strength of his sister's nephew, Philip IV of Spain.

The Bohemians had the backing of Norway, Sweden, Denmark, and much of the rest of the northern reaches of the Holy Roman Empire. They also gained the support of the Ottoman Empire, which, although an Islamic state, viewed the Catholics as their traditional enemies and opted to join forces with the Protestants.

The conflict initially went very badly for the Protestants. The first major battle of the war took place at White Mountain just outside of Prague in 1620. The imperial forces easily overran the Protestant forces and managed to gain control of Bohemia. This was a devastating blow to the German princes, who struggled to present a stable enough coalition to ward off the imperial troops.

A major development occurred in 1630 when Lutheran-believing Swedish Protestants took up an invitation from the embattled Protestants. They were not doing this so much out of their own goodwill to help the Protestants but rather to create a reliable buffer zone between them and imperial power.

The Swedes wished to make northern Germany a friendly pit stop and proxy just south of Sweden and the rest of Scandinavia. The Swedes made a direct alliance with Lutheran Saxony and Calvinist Brandenburg. This was a tenuous alliance since the Saxons and the people of Brandenburg did not want the Swedish king, Gustavus Adolphus, to get too powerful. They wanted the Swedes' help in pushing out imperial troops, but they did not want the Swedes to become the unquestioned power player as a result. In other words, they did not want to trade one bully for another.

Holy Roman Emperor Ferdinand II seemed to realize just how desperate the German Protestants were and decided to attempt some last-ditch bargaining with them. It was made known to the electors that the Edict of Restitution might be amended if all parties could somehow come to the table. The Protestants, as desperate as they were, were wary of bargaining with the emperor at this point. In April of 1631, after meeting at a Protestant assembly in Leipzig, they issued the Leipzig Manifesto, which stated their desire to defend their German Protestant liberties in the face of aggression.

The following month, forces of the Holy Roman Empire burned the Saxon city of Magdeburg to the ground. It has been said that some twenty thousand Protestants were killed. This only drove the Protestants and Swedes closer together, and in September of 1631, they scored a major win at the Battle of Breitenfeld. In this exchange, the Holy Roman Empire army suffered two deaths for every three soldiers that had been placed on the battlefield. This was a devastating blow for the Holy Roman Empire, which was having a hard enough time rallying its own troops.

By this point, the Swedes had made their way into Pomerania and Prussia. Even though they were allegedly fighting for the German Protestants, those same Protestants began to grow increasingly resentful of the Swedish presence on their soil. The Swedes would ultimately be pushed out. In September 1634, the Swedes and their Protestant allies were decimated by imperial troops. It is thought that some twelve thousand Protestants were killed in this exchange. This was enough to send the Swedes packing, and by November, they were leaving northern Germany.

Now that the Swedes were gone, the princes of northern Germany had to find a new ally. That new ally came in the unexpected form of Catholic France. This brings us to one of the most pivotal moments of this complicated and confusing decades-long debacle.

In 1635, France joined the conflict. This was done under the hand of France's infamous Cardinal Richelieu. France's actual ruler at this time was nine-year-old Louis XIII. A nine-year-old, of course, is not old enough to call the shots on their own, so France was governed by a core group of royal advisers until Louis XIII came of age.

Cardinal Richelieu was serving as the prime minister of France when the decision was made for French forces to get involved in the brewing conflict in Central Europe. Most would have assumed that the predominantly Catholic French would have sided with the Catholic forces of the Holy Roman Empire, but the French sided with the Protestants! This was pure and simple Machiavellian strategizing on the part of Richelieu, who, despite the fact of being a Catholic priest, could not resist the opportunity to inflict serious damage on one of France's major geopolitical rivals.

Just the mere thought of France weighing in like this was enough to make both sides consider possible negotiations. Shortly after this development, in May 1635, Saxony and Brandenburg's electors signed the Peace of Prague with the Holy Roman emperor. Known as a victory of pragmatism over religion, the Peace of Prague stipulated that the crown and the electors would work together to keep foreign powers, such as France, out of the conflict.

While the terms of this peace were still being hashed out, Holy Roman Emperor Ferdinand II perished in 1637. The interesting thing is that although peace was being made within the Holy Roman Empire, the former ally of northern Germany, Sweden, was beginning to get worried. It was in Sweden's best interest to keep imperial forces out of northern Germany to create a buffer zone. Sweden had to put its nose into these matters and stir up enough trouble to derail the peace process that had been started. France had similar concerns and was soon demanding to have certain stipulations met.

This led to extensive talks in 1641 in Münster and Osnabrück between imperial representatives (who stood in for German Protestants) and Sweden and France. These terms would be discussed over the next few years, and intermittent fighting continued to break out.

From our modern vantage point, it can be difficult to understand why it took so long to bring a complete end to the fighting. All sides wanted to stop the war at this point. Yet, it proved exceedingly hard for them to do so. Perhaps the best example of such a situation in more modern times is the Vietnam War. The war began between the French and the North Vietnamese immediately after the Second World War.

The French desperately fought the North Vietnamese insurgency until the US took over support for South Vietnam in the late 1950s. The US then began putting boots on the ground in the 1960s. The war quickly turned into an unwinnable quagmire, yet rather than de-escalating the conflict, the US sent more and more troops. By the 1970s, it was clear to just about everyone that the US had to end the war and get out of Vietnam.

Even so, the US could not just pull out overnight. Instead, what ensued was a very complicated set of negotiations on how the United States would exit Vietnam. These talks stretched on until the US finally left for good in 1975. The final phase of the Thirty Years' War produced a similar situation.

Just like in Vietnam, vested interests were at stake. Many sides had fought and suffered for several years, and they were so entrenched that no one knew how to pull their troops out easily. There was also the postwar state of Central Europe to consider. All of these things had to be hammered out in what would become the 1648 Peace of Westphalia.

This treaty had to satisfy all of those who had become involved. And for the most part, it did. It gave the Swedes some chunks of Pomerania, including important ports on the Baltic. This seemed to satisfy the Swedish demand for a buffer zone between it and the Holy Roman Empire. The French, for their part, were bought off by giving them some footholds along the Rhine, as well as the coveted regions of Alsace and Lorraine.

As for the German princes, they were given what they wanted in the first place. They were given the right to rule their immediate domain as they saw fit, and their Protestant subjects were free to remain Protestant. Another noteworthy development was the fact that Fredrick William, the great elector of Brandenburg-Prussia, was handed East Pomerania. This would be crucial in the development of a much more powerful state known as Prussia later on.

The Holy Roman emperor had been reduced to little more than a figurehead. The German princes had to recognize him as their overlord, but what exactly did that mean? The only real point that was stipulated to the German princes was not to get involved with foreign affairs that went against the wishes of the emperor.

So, the patchwork of German kingdoms within the Holy Roman Empire became even more autonomous than they had been before. It was a tenuous, fragile existence that was hatched out by the Peace of Westphalia, and it would not be long before the foreign intrigue that the German princes had been forbidden to engage in would threaten to tear the whole empire asunder.

Chapter 6: The Enlightenment and the Rise of Prussia

"The whole garrison of Berlin had turned out. A great show of princes, generals and so forth. I mingled with the crowd and was struck with the interest manifested by the lowest people in things military. Not a trace of the former animosity against the military which used to be noticeable among the lower classes. The commonest working man looked on the troops with the feeling that he belonged or had belonged to them."

-Prince Chlodwig zu Hohenlohe-Schillingsfürst[1]

The region we know today as Germany has been a center of commerce for thousands of years. Commercial goods and ideas have flowed freely throughout Europe and beyond due to Germany. This was the land that gave birth to Wolfgang Amadeus Mozart, Franz Joseph Haydn, Johann Sebastian Bach, Immanuel Kant, and Ludwig van Beethoven.

Intertwined with this increasing sense of culture and identity, the patchwork of states that made up the Holy Roman Empire were becoming more assertive and distinct in their own right. The Peace of Westphalia ensured further regional autonomy, leading to the rise of what chroniclers of German history have dubbed the Kleinstaaterei, or small stateships.

---

[1] Retallack, James. *Imperial Germany: 1871-1918.* 2008. Pg. 19.

The small states were in control of their own destiny and actively shaping their future. This was certainly the case as it pertained to powerful German states such as Bavaria, Saxony, Austria, and Brandenburg-Prussia. These regions were so autonomous that they had their own religious preferences, their own bureaucracy, and even their own armies.

The Holy Roman emperor was ostensibly considered the overlord of all of these principalities, but he was really just a peer among equals. He was barely able to keep it all together. The emperor of the Holy Roman Empire would soon find himself cast in Prussia's prominent shadow. At the dawn of the 1700s, Austria would form the base of the Holy Roman Empire, and the Habsburgs became the hereditary rulers.

At this time, Prussia had a population of just around three million. By the 1750s, Prussia boasted one of the region's strongest military forces and was expanding its borders. The bureaucracy of the Holy Roman Empire was huge and cumbersome. The main arbiter of disputes between the many parts of the empire was the imperial body known as the Reichstag. Although the Reichstag of this period did not have a fixed location, from 1664 to 1806, the Reichstag meetings most commonly convened in the Bavarian city of Regensburg. Individual states had their own bureaucratic machinery, but the larger, overarching Reichstag served the main purpose of vetoing direct decrees from the emperor. A similar analogy would be a US president or British prime minister consistently faced with a Congress or Parliament filled with members from the opposing party. The Holy Roman emperor was perpetually paralyzed unless he could somehow get the Reichstag to agree to go along with his bidding.

The emperor was also not well equipped to protect these principalities from outside threats. A prime example of this was the crisis of the Austrian succession, which morphed into the devastating Seven Years' War. This would prove to be one of the most pivotal wars of the century as it pertained to the fate of Central Europe. The reasons for the war are both simple and complex. The root of the conflict revolved around the succession of one would-be potentate, Maria Theresa, to the Austrian throne. However, the war becomes exceedingly complicated because of all of the motives of the other power players involved and the inevitable agendas that got mixed up in this whole mess.

Maria Theresa was the daughter of Holy Roman Emperor Charles VI, and she had the right to succeed her father as ruler of the House of Habsburg. Holy Roman Emperor Charles VI specifically set out a decree in 1713 known as the Pragmatic Sanction for this very purpose.[i] The decree stipulated that Maria Theresa could succeed her father if he had no male heir to the Austrian throne, which the Habsburgs had dominated for so long.

The Habsburgs were a dynastic family line that stemmed back to the rise of Rudolf I as king of Germany in 1273 CE. Rudolf acquired what was then known as the Dutchy of Austria, which was a principality of the Holy Roman Empire. In 1508, Holy Roman Emperor Maximilian I came to power. Maximilian was of the Habsburg line, and from here on out, the House of Habsburg would rule the Holy Roman Empire. The makeup of the empire changed when Maximilian gained control of the Netherlands by way of his marriage to Mary of Burgundy even though she perished before he officially became emperor.

This set the stage for further consolidation of the realm by Maximilian's grandson, Charles V, who was elected as the new Holy Roman emperor in 1519. Along with the lands he took over from Maximilian, Charles V ended up inheriting the Spanish throne and its colonies from his father, Philip the Handsome, who had married Joanna the Mad of Spain (yes, these are actual titles).

The domain that Charles V ended up controlling was mind-bogglingly large, and as such, he was constantly on the move from one part of the empire to another just to make sure that everything was in order. A weary, sick, and tired Charles V abdicated in 1556, allowing his son, Philip II of Spain, and his brother, Ferdinand I, to effectively split their inheritance. Ferdinand I gained Austria and other imperial holdings, while Philip was left with control of the Netherlands, part of Italy, and the vast Spanish Empire, which at that point controlled much of South America and parts of North America. He also controlled the Philippines, which was named after Philip, of course.

The Habsburgs centered around Austria controlled much of what had traditionally been the Holy Roman Empire, as well as additionally acquired lands in Eastern Europe. Charles VI, the father of Maria Theresa and whose succession caused the crisis, was both the Holy

---

[i] Middleton, John. *World Monarchies and Dynasties*. 2005. Pg. 360.

Roman emperor and the head of the vast Habsburg domain. Charles VI died on October 20th, 1740 without a male heir. There were those who believed that Maria Theresa should be allowed to succeed her father, but there were those who came out in clear opposition. All factions had their reasons behind either supporting or opposing Maria Theresa's succession. Those who supported her succession pointed to the Edict of Pragmatic Sanction, which had been issued by Charles VI and ensured that hereditary possessions could be inherited by a female heir if necessary.

However, this edict did not say that a female heir could become a Holy Roman empress. And since the Habsburgs had such a stranglehold on the office at this point, the succession of Maria Theresa created a quandary. Maria Theresa and her inner circle had a solution. It was proposed that she would not become Holy Roman empress; instead, her husband, Francis Stephen, would be elected as Holy Roman emperor.

Frederick II the Great, the leader of mighty Prussia, disagreed. Although no one to this day can say exactly what was in Frederick's heart, it has long been suggested that his ulterior motive in coming out in opposition to the succession was seizing Austrian Silesia, a wealthy province, for his own and incorporating it into Prussia. Frederick argued against Maria Theresa's succession and then made claims to Silesia.

Frederick II of Prussia.⁹

These developments kicked off the War of the Austrian Succession on December 16th, 1740. It was then up to all of the other great powers of the day to weigh in, depending on their own self-interests. And weigh in they did. Great Britain, the Netherlands, the Kingdom of Sardinia, and the Electorate of Saxony came out on the side of Maria Theresa. However, France supported Prussia.

Initially, it did not look too good for Prussia since Frederick's only reliable ally was the Electorate of Bavaria. However, Frederick's mighty army quickly won a series of stunning victories in the First Silesian War. The Prussians were skilled in warfare strategies and were notoriously good at pummeling the weakest enemy positions before forcing entire defensive lines to scatter. Frederick employed such a tactic during the bloody fighting at Mollwitz in 1741. In 1742, the Prussians scored another major victory.

By this time, Frederick was calling himself the king of Prussia. This was important because his father had gone by the more subservient title of king in Prussia. By stating that he was the king *of* Prussia (including the newly conquered lands in Austria), he was shaking off any notion that he was subordinate to any other overlord.

These hammer blows resulted in the Treaty of Breslau, which ceded Silesia and Glayz County to Prussia. Prussia then invaded Bohemia, kickstarting the Second Silesian War.

Frederick and his Prussian forces scored more wins in the second round of fighting, getting the best of the battles centered around Soor and Hohenfriedberg. These conquests in Silesia led to a virtual doubling in the size of Prussia's territory and boosted its overall revenue significantly as well.

All of these developments led to the 1745 Treaty of Dresden. This, again, forced Austria to recognize the Treaty of Breslau, but Frederick finally acknowledged Maria Theresa's husband as the rightfully elected Holy Roman emperor. However, Frederick's Prussia had unquestionably become a major player in Europe.

And Frederick, the man who had initiated the bloody conflict, was being hailed as "Great." Not since Charlemagne had a figure risen up with such vigor and audacity. Frederick was poised to take on the whole world. However, he was a pragmatic realist instead of a world conqueror. After coming out on the winning side of the Silesian wars, he knew that his hand had been fully played. He had won the wars, but it had come at a high cost in both blood and treasure, the latter of which he sought to replenish by utilizing the rich resources of the newly seized lands, as well as by raising taxes on his older domains.

Frederick was an absolutist. He believed that he should have absolute authority over his realm, but he also believed that he was an "enlightened" absolutist. This means that Frederick was an advocate of many of the ideals of the European Enlightenment, which had taken a firm hold on much of Western Europe at the time.

Although the Enlightenment is mostly considered the plaything of philosophers, it actually dovetails with the Scientific Revolution, which had begun just prior. The discoveries of great scientists, such as Johannes Kepler, Francis Bacon, Isaac Newton, and Galileo Galilei, managed to provoke the minds of many philosophers. Galileo, in particular, provoked them in a couple of ways. He proved that Earth is not the center of the universe.

Prior to Galileo's discovery that the Earth revolved around the sun and not the other way around, most people believed that the Earth was literally center stage. Everything revolved around it. This was a common misconception. When we look up into the skies, not realizing that the Earth is moving underneath our feet, it does appear as if the sun is rising and setting—that the sun is the one doing the moving and the Earth is standing still. Galileo's findings proved that this was not the case, and it was (for lack of a better word) earth-shattering, or at least it was enough to shatter some of humanity's hubris.

Another way a scientist like Galileo provoked the mind of the philosopher was the reaction of authoritarian rulers to their findings. Rather than celebrate Galileo's discovery, the authorities (both religious and secular) sought to suppress what Galileo had discovered. These social gatekeepers seemed to think that Galileo's revelation that Earth was not as unique as people had once thought was dangerous and needed to be kept from the public at all costs. They forced Galileo to recant his writings.

In the years that followed, philosophers began to reflect on these things and began to consider how damaging and stifling authoritarian gatekeepers of society could be to free thought and the advancement of human knowledge. It was in this way that the Scientific Revolution jumpstarted the Age of Enlightenment, which had the philosophically minded reconsider the structure of society and even human nature itself.

Soon, philosophers such as Thomas Hobbes, John Locke, Voltaire, and Rene Descartes explored the depths of the human soul to find answers to some of humanity's deepest questions. Ironically enough, these musings even resonated with later authoritarian rulers such as Prussia's Frederick the Great.

This led to a peculiar creation of leaders known as enlightened despots or enlightened absolutists. Some philosophers agreed with the concept. French philosopher Voltaire (who eventually befriended Frederick) was a well-known supporter of the notion of "philosopher kings."

At any rate, despite the carnage Frederick had unleashed, he truly believed that he—being the enlightened authoritarian despot that he was—had his people's best interests at heart and sought to create a state that would uplift the masses. Even so, by the eruption of the Third Silesian War in 1756, which would become a theater of the Seven Years' War, the notion that Frederick had his people's best interest at heart would become increasingly strained.

This war was a mixed bag for Prussia in the sense that the Prussians lost as many battles as they had won. Prussia saw incredible reversals, and on two different occasions, the mighty city of Berlin was occupied by enemy forces.

The year 1757 saw the worst defeat for the Prussians in the Battle of Kolín, which is said to have taken the lives of over nine thousand Prussian troops. Prussia rallied, and shortly thereafter, Prussian forces, even though facing numerically superior armies, scored two subsequent victories in the Battles of Rossbach and Leuthen, the latter of which left all enemy combatants on the field either dead or taken prisoner.

The Prussians scored another victory after this smashing win at the Battle of Zorndorf, but it was considered a Pyrrhic one. Although sixteen thousand Russians were killed or injured, as many as thirteen thousand Prussians were as well. Since Prussia, under normal circumstances, was not able to field an army as large as the Russians could, this "victory" was indeed a costly one.

The Prussians suffered a string of defeats from 1758 to 1759. The first defeat was the Battle of Hochkirch, which left one-third of Frederick's forces in ruins. The Battle of Kunersdorf was much worse since only a fraction of the Prussians involved were left alive. The army that went into the battle was some forty-eight thousand strong. It is said that some twenty thousand men were killed or injured. Even worse, it has been estimated that half a million civilians perished in all of this endless fighting.

The war ultimately came to a close by means of diplomacy. The war officially ended with the Treaty of Hubertusburg in 1763. The treaty basically returned all belligerents to their pre-war status quo. Even so, Prussia was the clear winner for being able to stand toe to toe with Austria without losing territory. By doing so, the Prussians demonstrated that they were a force to be reckoned with.

Once the fighting was over, Frederick tried his best to rebuild and remake Prussia into not only a military power but also a cultural power. He made Berlin a major city and enacted democratic reforms such as freedom of the press and fairly progressive social programs for his citizens.

Frederick began the process of codifying Prussian law in 1780. The laws in these legal books were progressive for the era. They reduced the reasons for capital punishment, forbade torture, and sought to stymie arbitrary arrests. Such things are rights that most of us take for granted in the Western world. But yes, before a nation like the United States had even fully fleshed out the Bill of Rights, Frederick was giving his people similar rights under his own legal code.

Chapter 7: The Napoleonic Era and the Confederation of the Rhine

Prussia's Frederick the Great, who had befriended French philosopher Voltaire, liked to style himself as an enlightened despot. However, he was still a despot. This was demonstrated at the end of the Seven Years' War. Upon hearing of the dismal figures of death and destruction, Frederick decided to "shoot the messenger." He was so irked by the findings that he is said to have had the bureaucrat who informed him of the sobering statistics put behind bars.

Even so, he was not nearly as despotic as the tyrants created by the French Revolution. Unlike what occurred in the United States of America and, most especially, France, the revolution that took place in the German states was relatively mild. America had to shake off the greatest power on the planet—Britain—in a bloody revolutionary war. France unleashed all sorts of inner demons in its quest to overthrow the French monarchy and establish a republic.

The Prussians reformed their country at a much more even keel. For one thing, they never sought to overthrow their monarch. Frederick's reforms might have been great, but he was also still great. The people accepted him as their ultimate leader and patiently waited for the reforms that he enacted. They certainly were not rushing to send old Frederick off to the guillotine anytime soon. The same could also be said of the later reign of Maria Theresa. She was a mild reformer, and her own people—if not her neighbors—accepted the pace with which she governed.

It was precisely due to the non-radical nature of the reforms that the German states had a lack of unity and purpose. They also lacked any real assurance that any individual rights they had gained would continue. The rights of freedom of religion granted in the past had been arbitrarily rescinded by monarchs—who was to say that such a thing could not occur again?

In the late 1700s and early 1800s, when the upheaval in France was occurring, the French seemed to be showing the Germans a potential pathway to becoming a modern, enlightened civilization. This was not the first time that the French had intervened in German history. The French had played a major role in the Thirty Years' War during the struggles revolving around the Austrian succession.

After France was turned upside down by its own revolution and especially after the rise of general-turned-dictator Napoleon Bonaparte, the French began to forcibly interfere with the German states even more. In the aftermath of the French Revolution, French troops entered German lands, announcing themselves as enlightened liberators.

The French were eagerly playing the role of enlightened big brothers in the cultural march toward modernity. The French essentially promised to speed up the process of the slow reforms offered by Habsburg monarchs in Austria and the Hohenzollern monarchs (such as good old Frederick) in Prussia.

The Germans were already fairly experienced in the business of revolutionary tumult since the German states were centerstage during the Reformation. Although the Protestant Reformation centered around and was cloaked by religion, it was a call for social reform as well. Since most of these efforts did not turn out as planned by the chief reformers, the Germans had it burned into their consciousness to take calls to reconstruct social norms with a fair amount of caution.

The one big thing that the German reforms and the French Revolution had in common was the fact that they both sought to limit the power of the central government's intrusion in personal affairs. The Germans had fought a long, hard fight to allow them to have some freedom of religion. The French Revolution, likewise, quickly put an end to state-sanctioned religion. That is until the revolutionaries briefly (and quite bizarrely) reversed course and attempted to create their own universal state religion. This was the design of the French revolutionary firebrand Maximilien Robespierre and would be exceedingly short-lived. Robespierre would eventually be executed. Ultimately, the French achieved a similar balance as the Germans, in which a limited amount of freedom of religion existed, free from the control of faraway religious leaders like the pope.

After the French Revolution erupted in 1789, the Germans began to wonder if perhaps they were not somehow behind when it came to the Enlightenment, which had swept across Western Europe. One person who seemed to ponder as much was the great German philosopher Immanuel Kant.

Kant looked toward the French and openly speculated. "Enlightenment is man's exodus from his self-incurred tutelage." In other words, enlightenment occurs when one seeks to leave the old pathways of tradition in order to discover new and more meaningful horizons.

Kant looked to his French brothers in philosophy, such as Voltaire and especially Jean-Jacques Rousseau. Rousseau was famous for stating his belief that "Everything is good when it leaves the hands of the [Creator], everything degenerates in the hands of man."[i]

Rousseau spoke of a very clear degeneration inherent in human civilization. French revolutionaries would need to correct this degeneration. French political intellectuals like Maximilien Robespierre agreed wholeheartedly that social institutions corrupted people and made otherwise good people bad. If those institutions were removed, humans could once again revert to their good, natural state.

However, back in Rousseau's day—and even today—the second the constructs of society, such as laws, a police force, and some sense of religious virtue, were removed, chaos was not far behind. Fans of Rousseau would learn the hard way that the institutions of society keep humans' worst inclinations in check, not the other way around.

Social rules and norms were created for a reason. Another great philosopher, Thomas Hobbes, was keen to point out that life would get pretty ugly, pretty fast, without laws. Rousseau thought that social

---

[i] Gibson, Andrew. *Modernity and the Political Fix*. 2019. Pg. 95.

institutions were the problem, but their removal would seemingly send humans back to the Stone Age. Whoever had the biggest club would be temporarily on top until someone with a bigger club came along. In short, such a society would not work. Without social institutions, the unchecked passions of the masses would run rampant.

Nevertheless, revolutionaries pointed to ideas spouted by Rousseau as gospel and their reasoning for doing what they did. The Bastille was stormed, and traditional leaders and representatives of society were put in chains.

Before things had turned quite so ugly, German philosophers were keen on borrowing ideas from French intellectuals. In the 1750s, under Frederick the Great, many in the Prussian court became Francophiles. Frederick loved all things French. He was fluent in both the language and the culture. Even so, Frederick believed that German culture was actually the better of the two. He believed that Germans had a tougher disposition and work ethic. They could make real and lasting change, whereas the French, as smart and ingenious as they were, were too weak-willed to really create anything of lasting importance.

Such things are noteworthy, considering Germany's later descent into madness under the Nazis, who also bragged about the strength of the German will. Even though the Nazis ran with this idea, it seems this had been a common theme in German society for many centuries. One could even argue that it dates back to the time of the Romans, who often cited the Germanic tribes they encountered as having a tenacious will.

Yet, the German barbarians of old worked hard to create society. Most of the leading lights of German society were not too thrilled in tearing society apart as the French revolutionaries suggested.

Frederick the Great was a free-thinking absolutist ruler, and he encouraged others to think for themselves. He even went as far as to have the Berlin Academy challenge its members to openly ponder the latest intrigues and philosophical musings. In 1780, just prior to his own passing, Frederick started a massive debate among the Germans over such complex concepts, such as whether it is useful to deceive people.

To many, such a question might seem wrong-footed from the start, but it is indeed a valid question for anyone interested in governing society. There are times when too much information, too soon, could cause more harm than benefit to the masses. Martin Luther famously opened up the floodgates by encouraging the laity to read the scriptures for themselves and find the truth of the Bible on their own. The results were cataclysmic. Without the Catholic Church handing down its own officially sanctioned interpretation, whole cities were fighting each other over their own perceived "truth" of the scripture. Considering all of this, one could rightfully argue and debate over just how much of the truth a government should tell its people.

We have examples of this approach actively in play today. If, for example, the United States military develops a cutting-edge stealth fighter that can maneuver in ways conventional aircraft could not, would they tell the public about it? Out of fears over national security, the public would be kept in the dark, especially in the initial stages of production, lest adversarial nations learn US secrets.

So, yes, as bad as it may seem at first glance, deceiving the public is often a matter of public policy.

German philosophical debate ultimately tended to side with solidarity with one's leader and one's nation. The notion of the "German nation" was a loose one since this was prior to the emergence of Germany as we know it today. However, the idea that society should ultimately defer to those in charge and show some sort of solidarity with the nation as a whole took hold among the German states in the aftermath of the French Revolution.

This could be viewed as the start of a kind of pseudo-German nationalism. The German states prized themselves for their cosmopolitan nature as the crossroads of Central Europe, but the threats from France caused a shift inward toward a more German nation.

The threat was enough to make the two leading lights of the German world, Frederick William II of Prussia and Austrian Habsburg ruler and Holy Roman Emperor Leopold II, join forces. This agreement to band together against the French occurred in 1790 at the Convention of Reichenback. The subsequent treaty was aimed at solidifying the budding coalition against revolutionary France.

A couple of years later, in 1792, the situation with France had reached a real tipping point, with French forces pushing right up to German borders. The German princes of the Rhine beefed up their previous agreement by entering into a mutual defense treaty with each other. France declared war on Austria in April 1792, and the French army subsequently rolled right into the Rhineland.

During this push, the French loudly proclaimed the liberation of several German cities, such as Worms, Mainz, and Speyer. A temporary wedge was made between the powers of Austria and Prussia, and the Prussians were convinced to remain neutral. The French continued to eat away at the Austrian side of the Holy Roman Empire, leading to a terrible defeat at Hohenlinden on December 3rd, 1800. This loss caused the Austrians to lose the western Rhineland.

By this point, Napoleon had already been declared emperor by the French and was determined to expand his imperial holdings. This unbridled ambition led to the stunning Battle of Austerlitz in 1805. Once again, Austria was delivered another terrible defeat.

The following year, in 1806, the Holy Roman Empire was dissolved. The reason for this dissolution was largely because Napoleon coerced the German princes of the Rhine to form the Confederation of the Rhine. After the Holy Roman Empire's dissolution, the Confederation of the Rhine came together even more. Prussia bore some guilt since it was a silent partner in all of this.

It did not take long for the Germans to realize just how terrible of a deal they had made. Some Germans likely felt they had made a deal with the devil, especially when it was realized in 1807 that Prussia, whose territory had already been gobbled up by the hungry French in the west, would end up losing even more. It was reduced to just its eastern holdings of Brandenburg, East Prussia, and Silesia.

Was this what Prussia was to be reduced to? Frederick the Great had fought hard to gain Silesia, but now, the Prussians had lost just about everything else. Prussia had been rendered into an ineffective rump state to serve French interests.

This situation would not stand for long. Germans were more determined than ever to stand together lest they fall prey to foreign depredations. The march toward German unification had just begun.

Chapter 8: Revolution to Unification

"German culture is above all the unity of artistic style in every expression of the life of a people."

-Frederich Nietzsche[1]

The French Revolution and its subsequent dictatorial conquest by Napoleon Bonaparte would end in disaster for the French. After running roughshod through Central Europe, the French dared to venture into the frigid depths of Russia. They arrived in Moscow in December 1812 only to find the city abandoned and everything burned to the ground.

The Russian army, which had relocated farther east, had set a trap for the unwary French. They had left a scorched and frozen earth behind them. The French tried to set up shop in the Russian capital but found that they were ill prepared for the winter. Without proper supplies and under constant attack by insurgents, they had to withdraw.

This led to a disastrous retreat across thousands of miles of snowy terrain that would leave Napoleon's army in shambles. The French were then dealt a terrible blow at the Battle of the Nations in Leipzig in 1813 by a combined force of British, Russians, and Prussians.

The French were forced to negotiate the terms of their surrender at the Peace of Paris in 1814. Napoleon was arrested. He would briefly

---

[1] Retallack, James. *Imperial Germany: 1871-1918*. 2008. Pg. 107.

escape and cause trouble again in 1815, but it was a lost cause. He would once again be defeated, and this time, he remained in exile for the rest of his life.

Because of all this tumult, the German states had changed. They were now on a new trajectory toward unification. If anything, they knew that the more united they were, the less likely some outside force could shake them asunder. Other world powers were not so certain that a united Germany was in their best interests. They sought to confound or at least delay these developments. The great powers supported a much less robust version of the German Confederation of the Rhine. The legislative center for this new amalgamation of German states was Frankfurt. This divided realm was much more palatable to the great powers of Britain, France, and Russia.

The culture and society of the realm began to see a throwback to classic social structures. The postwar period of the 1820s has been ridiculed by some antagonists as the Biedermeier era. The Biedermeier era was really a mixed bag. It was an era that valued the upper middle class, but their status was not locked in. During this period, German society valued meritocracy and a strong work ethic. Those who were deemed to have worked hard enough could rise up to the middle class or beyond.

The Biedermeier era kept old societal values close to heart yet championed what historian Steven E. Ozment has described as an upwardly mobile society of innovative thinkers in which merit was prized over aristocratic heritage.[i] Yes, the Germans tried to have it both ways. They wished for strong law and order, conservative values, a love of king and country, and rapid mobility based upon meritocratic skill rather than birth. Anyone could be anything they wanted as long as they obeyed the king, worked hard, and proved their worth in whatever trade they applied themselves to.

Despite the disdain of its critics, the Biedermeier era proved to be immensely appealing to many, both inside and outside of Germany. Perhaps it is just human nature for people to eventually want more because those who benefited the most from this situation—the German middle class—ended up championing the revolutionary reforms that began in the 1830s.

---

[i] Ozment, Steven. *A Mighty Fortress.* 2004.

In 1830, the July Revolution broke out in France. As we mentioned earlier, the French had greatly influenced German life and culture since the days of Roman Gaul and Germania. This sign of unrest in France led to the lands of Germany bracing themselves for homegrown unrest. Police in several states, including Saxony, Hannover, Bavaria, and Baden, put their officers on high alert.

They had good reason to be on their guard. Around this time, a new movement of German reformers, called the Young Germany movement, was getting ready to push their luck with the German government. Protesters mobilized in the 1840s, demanding changes such as open elections, universal voting for men, reform of the courts, and greater freedom of speech, press, and religion. These protests were fueled by further problems in 1846. A downturn in the economy and problems with certain crops vital to the vast bulk of Germans led to increasing levels of unrest.

Under this pressure, the loose confederation of German states began calling for a greater sense of unity by way of a national parliament and perhaps even a national constitution. This tumult had apparently reached a tipping point by March 1848. The disturbance became so great that the chief minister of affairs in Austria, Prince Metternich, fled to England, and Emperor Ferdinand I of Austria was run right out of Vienna.

In the meantime, King Frederick William IV of Prussia was in his palace as protests erupted all around him. Feeling decidedly backed into a corner, he began to make certain concessions to the protesters, but as is often the case, this acquiescence only added fuel to the fire. He soon found himself essentially under house arrest. While he was being confined in his palace, he was pressured by the reformers to approve the election of a brand-new parliament. The new national parliament first met on May 18th, 1848, in St. Paul's Church in the city of Frankfurt. The debates over the constitution continued into 1849 until what Steven E. Ozment describes as a kind of "rump parliament" was established in Stuttgart that June.[1] These gatherings typically consisted of 450 delegates from the middle class. This group clamored for reform but called for moderation. There was a balancing act at play between individual freedoms and the overarching authority of the state. Although the

---

[1] Ozment, Steven. *A Mighty Fortress*. 2004.

middle class was overrepresented, the members of parliament were cognizant of the lower classes and crafted legislation with them in mind.

These delegations became the voice of a proto-German state. This voice was seeking something akin to a constitutional monarchy in which the monarch had a more limited role than had been enjoyed in the past. But who would that monarch even be? A Habsburg? A Hohenzollern? Some believed that the best path forward would be to create a smaller state under the authority of Prussian King Frederick William IV.

However, Fredrick William was not thrilled about it. He remarked that any crown that the revolutionaries might give him would essentially be a dog collar. Rather than reigning, he would be reined in by the restraints placed on him by the revolutionaries.

At any rate, on April 3rd, 1849, when the assembly extended Frederick William an offer of a crown, he insisted that all of the kings, princes, and free cities of the empire be polled on how they felt about it first. Ultimately, he refused to accept their offer. Unable to convince Frederick William and unable to gain wider international recognition, the Frankfurt National Assembly fell apart. Its Prussian counterpart followed suit in May.

In the aftermath of all this, the dynamic figure of Otto von Bismarck began to rise to prominence. While no one can deny his importance to German history, the legacy of Bismarck has continued to divide the opinions of historians. It was under Bismarck that Germany first became a nation in its own right. Bismarck was crucial in Germany achieving this, but it is here that the political divide begins. Some argue that Bismarck stymied the modernization of Germany and the Enlightenment ideals that had begun many years before, while others argue that Bismarck was the steward of the Germans as they entered into the modern age.

Interestingly, if one were to look at Bismarck's personal background, one would see that his family life growing up was similarly divided. His dad lived the rather lackadaisical life of a Junker—that is, the relatively easy lifestyle of the property-holding elite of Prussia. His mother was more industrious. Living the life of a landlord was not fulfilling enough for her. Her ambition influenced her son to move away from the easy life of the aristocracy toward a life as an industrious civil servant for the bustling meritocracy.

Bismarck ended up at some of the top schools in Berlin. He graduated and succeeded in entering the civil service, but he initially did not take to it very well. Soon, he started to look fondly at the traditional aristocratic stylings of the Junkers.

While he kept one foot in the world of the aristocratic property owners of Prussia and the other in the world of civil service, his fortunes slowly but steadily began to rise. In 1848, Bismarck, from his post in the Prussian Diet, pushed back against the more radical reformers. His efforts were recognized by the Prussian powers, and from here on out, he was an in-demand pick for ministerial positions.

In 1851, Bismarck was made Prussia's official envoy to the German Confederation based out of Frankfurt. During his time in Frankfurt, Bismarck downplayed some of his previous rhetoric that had placed him in stiff opposition to much of the reforms. He became more of a pragmatist and began to adopt a moderate stance that he hoped would take Germany down a middle road somewhere between the two poles of conservative caution and liberal abandon.

Although Bismarck was initially opposed to German unification, he became more and more accepting—even encouraging—of the push toward it. Bismarck, true to his own pragmatic sense of realpolitik, which he would later make so famous, seemed to think that unification was inevitable and that it would be better served with the aristocratic Junker class at the helm rather than the most extreme revolutionaries.

Bismarck would become increasingly immersed in international politics. He —was an ambassador to Russia in 1859 and then an ambassador to France in 1862. During his time in France, he got a clear view of Napoleon III's government.

Napoleon III would later lead the French nation into a war with the Germans, just as his namesake, Napoleon I, had done several decades prior. Napoleon III had risen to power in France during the 1848 tumult that had rocked much of Europe. He had since eschewed democratic elections in favor of reigning as a popular despot and dictator over what was declared a new French Empire.

Perhaps this increasing threat of a reinvigorated France had Bismarck consider unification as not just a matter of reform but also of national security. Napoleon Bonaparte had thoroughly taken advantage of German disunity and managed to destroy the Holy Roman Empire. He almost destroyed the Prussian and Austrian kingdoms as well. Germany needed to be unified to stand up to such threats, and it was likely with all of this in mind that Bismack went on the record in September of 1862 to state that Germany must be unified not by speeches and deliberation but by "blood and iron."

Strategic territorial changes were happening in the meantime. In November 1863, King Frederick VII of Denmark's passing instigated a dispute over the duchies of Holstein and Schleswig. Frederick VII's heir, Christian IX, was in the process of claiming them, but his claims were disputed by a Danish duke named Frederick von Augustenburg.

The Prussians came out on the side of the Danish duke, hoping to gain territory for themselves in the process. Bismarck was cautious about weighing in, but after Christian IX unilaterally annexed the territory, Prussia, with Austrian support, waged war against Denmark. The Prussian-Austrian coalition won and forced Christian IX to relinquish his claims.

Since the Prussians and Austrians were ostensibly supporting Danish Duke Augustenburg, one would think that the spoils would go to him as well. However, Prussia and Austria had other plans, which were made known by way of the Gastein Convention in 1865. Prussia was given control of Schleswig, and Austria gained control of Holstein.

Austria eventually went back on this treaty, which sparked a war between Prussia and Austria. The two sides came to a cataclysmic clash in Bohemia at the Battle of Königgrätz. The Austro-Prussian War ultimately ended with the 1866 Treaty of Prague, which led to the Austro-Hungarian Compromise the following year. The compromise saw the establishment of Austria-Hungary.

The year 1867 also saw the establishment of the North German Confederation. Bismarck played a big part in this new confederation of German states. He helped draft its constitution and would be appointed as its chancellor.

Prussia's western flank was significantly threatened by Napoleon III with the outbreak of the Franco-Prussian War in 1870. By this time, Otto von Bismarck had risen to the post of chancellor and had a front-row seat to all of the intrigue that led up to the war. France had been caught off guard by the stunning Prussian victory against Austria, and in many ways, it was itching for a fight. Bismarck, as astute as he was, realized as much.

It all started in 1870 when one of Prussian King William's family members—Prince Leopold of Hohenzollern-Sigmaringen—was asked to take over the Spanish throne, which had been empty since the tumult of the Glorious Revolution, which had taken place in Spain in 1868. Post-revolutionary Spain had limped along with a provisional government after deposing its Queen Isabella. But by 1870, the Spanish had begun sending invitations to Prince Leopold to see if he would take the helm of a constitutional monarchy.

This set off alarm bells in France since such a move would essentially have the French surrounded by German powers. The French complained about this to Prussia. At first, King William was conciliatory and considerate of France's concerns and was persuaded to discourage his relative from taking the Spanish up on their offer. However, when the French got a little too pushy and essentially demanded the Prussians pledge never to have any of their royal family members accept the crown for Spain, the Prussian king began to become agitated.

King William rejected this last request. The king's official missive fell into the lap of Bismarck to deliver, and he was crafty enough to take advantage of an explosive political situation. He knew that the French were saber-rattling, and Bismarck predicted that if a fight was to be had, the French would have to lose. So, he decided to do some last-minute revising of the king's letter to make it even more upsetting to the French to see if he could push them into war. He purposefully deleted any pleasantries and embellished any hints of aggression. He hoped that the harshness of the words would set the French off and make them want to fight. His letter revising scheme was a stunning success.

By July 1870, the French and the Prussians were fighting. The war did not go at all well for the French, and after months of bloody fighting, the Prussians were on the doorstep of Paris. French military units laid down their arms at Metz and Sedan, and the French were forced to capitulate. The French defeat resulted in the Prussians laying claim to the coveted regions of Lorraine and Alsace. Along with this land grab, the Prussian victors also made France fork over some five billion francs in reparations.

The French eventually made good on the terms of the treaty and paid back all that was demanded. The French would not forget this punitive measure and paid it back to the Germans a hundredfold when the Prussian successor state of Germany was defeated in World War One.

German nationalism had reached an undeniable high point after the victorious conclusion of the Franco-Prussian War. The lands of Germany, despite all odds, were coming together as one nation.

Bismarck led the negotiations to make unification a reality. On January 18th, 1871, William (or Wilhelm) I of Prussia was made German emperor. Twenty-five German states united and saw the king of Prussia, now the German emperor, as their overlord. Bismarck was made the imperial chancellor of this new German Empire, or Reich as the Germans called it. Even so, Bismarck knew all too well that the international stage was quite precarious. There were still the dangers posed by a resentful France in the west, as well as the threat of intrigue from Russians in the east. Britain was unpredictable, as it freely entered into alliances with both powers.

A map of the German Reich.[10]

As such, Bismarck took a slow, cautious approach. His pragmatic caution irked Wilhelm I's successor, Wilhelm II, who rose to the throne of German emperor (or Kaiser) in 1888. Kaiser Wilhelm II had much greater ambition than his father and began to push for a more proactive German policy. This desire for more robust maneuvering on the world stage led him to force the aging Bismarck into retirement in 1890.

Kaiser Wilhelm II ramped up his aggressive imperial ambition by establishing colonies in Africa and Asia. Prior to this point in history, Germany had been largely left out of the colonial game that saw Britain, France, Spain, and even Italy seize extraterritorial possessions abroad. Kaiser Wilhelm was determined to establish what German colonies he could while he still had a chance.

During this scramble for colonies, the Kaiser made sure to beef up the German navy. This sparked a bit of an arms race with the British Empire; this arms race would continue all the way up until the outbreak of World War One.

The Kaiser's policies with its once reluctant ally, Austria-Hungary, would set the political stage on fire just enough to spark the conflagration of the First World War.

Chapter 9: The World Wars: Turmoil and Transformation

"Sir, this is Patton talking. The past fourteen days have been straight hell. Rains, snow, more rain, more snow—and I am beginning to wonder what's going on in your headquarters. Whose side are you on anyway?"

-General George S. Patton's prayer to God[i]

By the dawning of the 20th century, a resurgent Germany had much of the world worried. In the east, the Russians were concerned about what a more powerful and ever-expanding German state in the middle of Central Europe might mean for them. The British were locked in an arms race with the Germans, as both sought to dominate the high seas. The French had a long history of conflict with German states and had good reason to anticipate further aggression on the horizon.

These reservations led the three great powers of Russia, Britain, and France to forge a binding alliance to counterbalance the German Empire and its erstwhile ally, Austria-Hungary. Soon, mutual defense treaties were enacted that stated that an attack on one would be an attack on all.

Today, it seems easy to point out the folly of these treaties since we all know that this set the stage for World War One. However, at the same time, we are not that far removed from history. It could be argued that

---

[i] O'Reilly Bill. *Hitler's Last Days: The Death of the Nazi Regime and the World's Most Notorious Dictator.* 2015. Pg. 148.

NATO (the North Atlantic Treaty Organization) could lead to a similar entanglement. NATO's charter states that an attack on one is an attack on all. So, one could reasonably ask the question, how is that different from the entangled alliances that led to World War One?

In the years before World War One, many feared that some sort of armed confrontation would erupt. Many feared that it would occur between British and German ships. It was also feared that such an exchange would trigger a larger conflict.

Rather than a clash of arms between two antagonistic navies cruising through waters, World War One began in the Balkans in 1914. It was sparked by a terrorist act. Archduke Franz Ferdinand was visiting Austria-Hungary's holdings in Bosnia when he and his wife were assassinated by a Bosnian-Serb radical who was part of the Black Hand, a Serbian nationalist group. This event triggered the trap that would send the great powers on a collision course to war.

This was the trigger, but the factors that led the world to be on the brink of war are much more complicated. For decades (one could even argue centuries) prior to the assassination of Archduke Franz Ferdinand, unreasonable and entangling alliances had been put into place. There was also a resurgent sense of nationalism at work, which made the situation even more explosive.

Austria-Hungary had come into existence as a result of the Compromise of 1867, which bound the two crowns together. This compromise was made to avoid lingering territorial questions in the region between Austria and Hungary since Hungary, although within the Austrian Empire, was allowed to express its own nationalist ambitions by being granted a certain degree of autonomy. Hungary had its own parliament and oversaw its own internal affairs.

However, even though the merger of Austria and Hungary might have avoided a potential conflict between Austria and Hungary, more territorial questions would emerge in the following decades, the most pressing of which was centered around the Balkans.

Many parts of the Balkans had recently gained independence before the assassination. Prior to doing so, this part of the world had been dominated by the Islamic powerhouse known as the Ottoman Empire. The Ottomans originated from a Turkic tribe that fought its way into Asia Minor during the Middle Ages. They proved quite formidable and began skirmishing with the Greek Byzantines, who controlled much of the region. The Ottomans ultimately prevailed against the Greeks and captured the Byzantine capital of Constantinople in 1453, transforming it into modern-day Istanbul, Turkey. The Turks were not done, though. They marched right into the Balkans, taking control of Bulgaria, Albania, Macedonia, Serbia, Bosnia, Herzegovina, Montenegro, and even Greece itself.

It was not until the 1800s that these conquered nations began to shake the Ottomans off. Greece broke free of the Ottomans in 1823, and Bulgaria did the same in 1885. However, not every Balkan country enjoyed a clean-cut independence movement. Bosnia, for example, merely traded one empire for another. It was ripped from the Ottomans' grip in 1878, only to be placed directly under the control of the Austro-Hungarian Empire.

Many Bosnian Serbs were not happy with this arrangement. They were upset at being under the rule of the Austro-Hungarian monarchy. This discontent gave rise to strong feelings of nationalism. This resurgence of nationalism led to a Bosnian-Serb nationalist gunning down Archduke Franz Ferdinand.

After the archduke's assassination, the Austrians began to make increasingly draconian demands on Serbia. Serbia feared aggression and began mobilizing troops. Germany promised Austria its full support in any potential conflict. With Germany's backing, Austria declared war on Serbia after Serbia refused to submit to all of Austria's demands.

Shortly thereafter, Russia came to Serbia's aid. Germany made good on its pledge to support Austria and returned the favor by declaring war on Russia. Russia, Britain, and France all eventually declared war on Germany. Germany shored up its allies of Austria-Hungary and the Ottoman Empire, the latter of which joined the war in October 1914.

Western Europe quickly turned into the front lines of a battlefield. The Germans had long feared having to fight a two-front war, but now faced with Russians in the east and the British and the French in the west, they had no choice but to do so. German war planners enacted the Schlieffen Plan. The plan, named after its architect, Field Marshal Alfred von Schlieffen, had been conceived a decade prior, in 1905. Schlieffen died in 1913, a full year before the outbreak of World War One in 1914. Schlieffen's plan called for a concentrated drive of German armed forces through Belgium and then straight south to Paris in order to deal a knockout blow to the French. This would allow the Germans to concentrate all of their armed might against the Russians in the east.

The only problem with this was that it meant Germany would have to violate international norms by invading neutral Belgium. Prior to invading, the Germans petitioned the Belgian government to give them permission to move troops through its territory. Since Belgium was determined to remain neutral, the Belgians refused to concede to these demands. Not willing to take no for an answer, the German Army forced its way into Belgium.

The Schlieffen plan would not turn out as well as was hoped. Britain joined the war once Belgium was invaded. The German forces stalled and came to a stop in France, still quite far from the French capital of Paris. The German forces dug in their heels by literally digging trenches. The infamous trench warfare of the Western Front saw both sides locked in a bloody stalemate of endless fighting, with neither side giving much ground. The lines were clearly drawn by long trenches, which were topped off with barbed wire. Both sides made use of the latest industrial tools of death and destruction, such as machine guns, hand grenades, and even chemical weapons.

While the conflict on the Western Front stalled, the Germans made considerable gains on the Eastern Front. Led by German war hero Paul von Hindenburg, the German armed forces pounded away at an increasingly unstable and ill-equipped Russian Imperial Army. The Germans were further aided by political chaos in Russia. The Russian Revolution erupted in 1917 and was followed by a communist takeover. The communists had no interest in continuing to fight a war that had been launched by the now-deposed Russian tsar and sought to end it. This resulted in the Treaty of Brest-Litovsk in March 1918. This ended German fighting in the east and renewed hope among many Germans that the war could be won in the west.

However, this was not to be. The Americans joined the conflict, and the Western Allies continued to hammer the Germans on the Western Front. The German Army was low on both morale and supplies. The German government was forced to see the writing on the wall. The German high command capitulated, Wilhelm II abdicated, and the 1919 Treaty of Versailles went into effect.

The treaty that ended World War One is important because, in many ways, its harsh terms led to World War Two. The treaty led to painful territorial losses, such as the ceding of Alsace-Lorraine to France and the loss of Danzig (modern Gdansk). Allied forces actively continued to occupy the Rhineland that bordered Germany and France, a sight that would be a continuous eyesore for Germans in the years to come. The German military was forced into a state of disarmament. But even worse were the reparations that France demanded, which would essentially bankrupt the already struggling German economy. There was no consideration of these things at the end of the war; the Allied forces had lost a lot of men fighting the Germans, and they wanted punitive damages.

Germany was being made into a pariah, and there was not much hope of escaping the situation. Radical German politicians would use these feelings of desperation and anger to gain momentum among the disillusioned German masses.

However, it would take some time for these dark undercurrents to surface. The government that succeeded the toppled German Empire of Wilhelm II was far different from what these postwar malcontents would come up with. In 1919, on the heels of the Treaty of Versailles, a fairly liberal and forward-thinking republic, the Weimar Republic, was founded.

The Weimar Republic was a strange mix of socialism and conservatism. This socially conscious republic sought to aid its economically depressed citizens, while certain factions called for a return to the Germany of old.

In the middle of all this, the Communist Party of Germany was founded. The communists were inspired by the Russian Revolution of 1917 and attempted to spark something similar in Germany. They pushed to topple the Weimar Republic in 1919. They failed, but that same year, another disaffected German by the name of Adolf Hitler latched onto a radical group called the National Socialist German Workers' Party (better known as the Nazi Party today).

Hitler was a former artist-turned-soldier who had fought in World War One. He believed that Germany had been betrayed from the inside by conniving bureaucrats, and he sought to turn Jews into scapegoats. Jewish people had lived in Central Europe for centuries and had assimilated well into German society by the 20th century. Yet, Hitler was trying his best to paint them as both the ultimate outsiders and the ultimate insiders. They were outsiders in the sense that they were portrayed as not being true Germans, even if their families had roots that went all the way back to the days of the Holy Roman Empire. Hitler and his Nazi cronies also described the Jews as dastardly insiders. They said Jews were so well connected with the governmental machinery of Germany that they had stabbed Germany in the back during World War One by pulling the strings behind the scenes and pushing for an armistice.

Hitler, high on this vicious rhetoric, led his angry followers in the Beer Hall Pusch of 1923, which attempted to overthrow the Weimar Republic. This push, just like the communist attempt a few years prior, failed miserably, and Hitler and his henchmen were either arrested or driven into exile.

The conditions in the Weimar Republic deteriorated considerably after the stock market crash of 1929. The global economic depression is better known by Americans as the Great Depression. The Germans were discontent and desperate for something positive. In this backdrop, a recently pardoned Adolf Hitler made a surprising comeback. It is not often that someone could be thrown in prison for plotting a coup only to be pardoned and completely rehabilitated in the eyes of the public. However, this was what happened with Hitler. The man who had been previously tried as a traitor was now viewed by many as a patriot.

This time around, Hitler decided that he and the Nazi Party would not try to overthrow the government by force but through the ballot box. The Nazi Party ran for election and ended up winning big in the 1932 election. The Nazis won a third of the vote, making them a true power player in the Reichstag (the German Parliament).

Those who were most vulnerable to Nazi aggression—the Jews of Germany—watched these events in horror. For many, the writing on the wall was already quite clear. Many of those who were able to do so were already planning a possible exodus from Germany. Among them was an esteemed physicist by the name of Albert Einstein.

Germany had become a hub of great and profound scientific minds in the first few decades of the 20th century, with notable figures such as Max Planck, Werner Heisenberg, and Albert Einstein—just to name a few—coming to great prominence for their remarkable scientific findings. Einstein was of Jewish heritage, and he sensed what the rise of the Nazi Party might mean. He did not waste any time making arrangements to make his own exit from the country before it was too late. He and his wife Elsa left Germany on December 10th, 1932, and never looked back.

Because of the intolerance of the Nazi Party, Albert Einstein never returned to the land of his birth.

On January 30th, 1933, Adolf Hitler became the chancellor of Germany. This made him the second-most powerful person in Germany after the aging president, Paul von Hindenburg. On February 27th, 1933, a young Dutchman by the name of Martin van der Lubbe attempted to set the Reichstag ablaze.

Although some historians have debated his motives, he was apparently a communist sympathizer. Whatever the case may be, Hitler used this terrorist attack as an excuse to declare a state of emergency and convinced Hindenburg to grant him emergency powers by way of the Enabling Act, which essentially made him dictator. Hindenburg would die the following year, and Hitler remained in complete control.

Hitler further cemented his grip on German society by silencing any opposition to his regime. In the summer of 1934, during what was termed the "Night of the Long Knives," there was an internal purge. Hitler and his subordinate Heinrich Himmler, who headed the SS (Schutzstaffel) and the Gestapo, began targeting another arm of Nazi enforcers known as the SA (Sturmabteilung). The SA was an older paramilitary group of the Nazi Party dating back to the 1920s. Its leader, Ernst Röhm, played a major role in helping Hitler's rise to power but had since fallen out of favor. Hitler was trying to gain the full support of Germany's armed forces at the time, and most of the top brass did not look too favorably on the SA, whose members were known to be disorderly, drunken thugs at best and all-out criminals at worst.

German generals and admirals wanted Hitler to get rid of them, and Hitler was willing to do so if it meant he gained the support of the German military. The SS took over the offices of the SA, and Henrich Himmler became Reichsführer of the SS, paving a path for his own rise to power within the Nazi hierarchy. The Nazis justified the purge by suggesting that Röhm and the SA were plotting to overthrow the government.

With the military on his side, Hitler began to rearm the German government. By 1935, Germany was in clear violation of the Treaty of Versailles, as German aircraft had been deployed in the skies over Germany. The following year, 1936, saw German troops head into the Rhineland. The Allied powers silently looked on.

This kickstarted a process of appeasement that would last until Germany invaded Poland in 1939. Although the world stood idly by for land grabs, the invasion of Poland could not be ignored. Britain and France declared war on Germany, and Germany returned the favor. World War Two had officially begun.

Unlike World War One, this conflict did not begin as a two-front war for the Germans. In the first phase of World War Two, the Germans did not have to fight the Russians on the Eastern Front. On the contrary, the Russians were working with them. Before the invasion of Poland, the German government signed a non-aggression pact with Soviet Russia. Unbeknownst to the rest of the world, there was a secret provision in the pact that agreed to a division of Poland. As a result, Poland was divided in two; the Germans occupied western Poland, and the Soviets set up shop in eastern Poland.

With their eastern flank secure, in 1940, the German war machine rolled north into Denmark and Norway before heading west into the Netherlands and Belgium. Yes, the Germans were once again cutting through Belgium to get to France, but unlike World War One, the German war machine would not stall out in a wasteland of trenches. On the contrary, the German forces would deal France a knockout blow.

Right as France was on the verge of capitulation, Italy entered the war on the side of Germany, declaring war on an already practically defeated France on June 10th, 1940. On June 25th, 1940, the French capitulated to the Germans and signed an armistice.

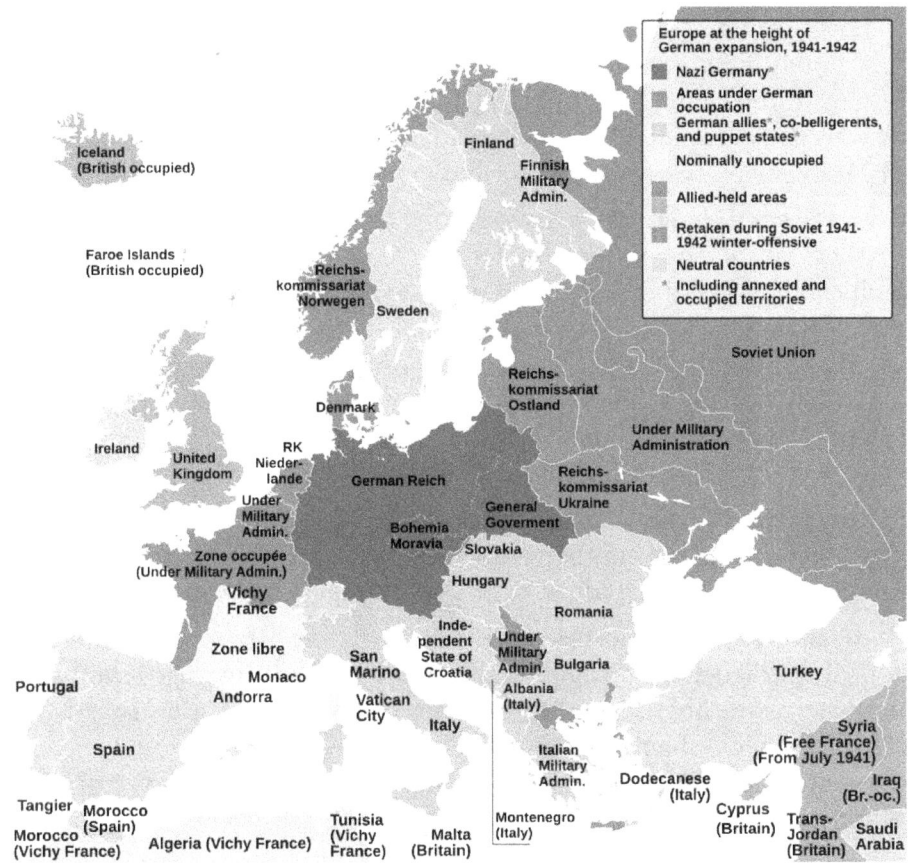

Height of German expansion in Europe.[11]

Britain became the only power left standing in the way of complete German domination of Western Europe. The Germans launched a brutal air war against Britain, which would become known as the Battle of Britain. However, British defenses proved surprisingly effective, and the Germans ultimately scrapped their plans to invade Britain. Frustrated with the British resistance, Hitler began looking east. In June of 1941, he did the unthinkable by double-crossing the Russians. Under the codename Operation Barbarossa, a war against Soviet Russia was unleashed. Initially, the Germans made tremendous gains. The Russians were caught by surprise and were pushed far back into the interior.

In the meantime, Germany's other ally, Japan, rocked the boat when it suddenly launched an unprovoked attack on a US naval base in Pearl Harbor, Hawaii. The attack occurred on December 7th, 1941. This incident finally dragged the United States into World War Two.

The Germans, in their push east, drove all the way to Moscow, but with supply lines stretched to their breaking point, they could go no further. In the summer of 1942, the Germans tried to drive farther south to seize the rich oilfields of the Russian Caucus. Doing so would have solved their supply line problem.

However, the German Army groups tasked with this feat would be smashed at Stalingrad. By this time, the United States had made significant inroads both against Japan and against German and Italian Axis forces in North Africa and the Mediterranean, further sealing Germany's doom. With the Germans making a slow, bloody retreat from the east, the Allies poured in from the west, landing in German-occupied Normandy, France, on June 6th, 1944.

The German forces would continue to get squeezed from both sides until they were finally forced to surrender in May 1945. Germany had been defeated in yet another world war, and the mad architect of this drama, Adolf Hitler, was dead in a Berlin bunker of an apparent suicide.

Hitler died alongside his newlywed wife, Eva Braun, on April 30th, 1945. He killed himself right as the Allies were closing in. True to his obstinate nature, he refused to take any blame for the catastrophe that had befallen Germany. In his so-called last will and testament, he did everything he could to try and remove any responsibility from his shoulders.

This final missive, penned by Hitler just one day prior to his suicide, was later found stuffed inside the bottom of a briefcase that had been tossed down a well. It had been apparently placed there by a man named Wilhelm Zander, who was one of the aides of Hitler's subordinate, Martin Bormann.[i]

Adolf Hitler's final will and testament contains his flat-out refusal to take responsibility for any of his actions. As Hitler put it, "I myself and my wife—in order to escape the disgrace of deposition or capitulation—choose death. It is our wish to be burnt immediately on the spot where I have carried out the greatest part of my daily work in the course of twelve years' service to my people."[ii]

---

[i] O'Reilly Bill. *Hitler's Last Days: The Death of the Nazi Regime and the World's Most Notorious Dictator.* 2015. Pgs. 453-454.

[ii] O'Reilly Bill. *Hitler's Last Days: The Death of the Nazi Regime and the World's Most Notorious Dictator.* 2015. Pg. 456.

Despite all of Hitler's denials, it was only after the war's end that the full horrors of the Holocaust would be made known. Prior to this, the outside world had only mere glimpses of the hostility that Hitler's regime had unleashed.

Although the full extent was not known, there had been some clear indicators that abusive measures had been taken against Jewish residents. Disturbing incidents such as Kristallnacht, or "Night of Broken Glass," in which Jewish businesses were destroyed and Jewish residents were harassed, had managed to make the international press.

This event occurred on November 9th, 1938. It was a heinous act of supposed collective punishment after a staff member of the German Embassy in Paris was murdered by a Jewish German. This first onslaught of hatred against the Jews actually did not go over as well as the Nazis had hoped. There were many Germans who were alarmed at what was happening. Perhaps they were not alarmed enough to really put a stop to it, but it was just enough to make the Nazis become a bit more discreet over how they conducted their persecution of people groups.

Once the Nazis had full control of their domain, they made sure to cover their tracks, and the full extent of what was happening was kept quiet. Jews were being loaded on train cars and sent to concentration camps. The average German did not quite understand what the fate of their Jewish neighbors actually was. This, of course, is no excuse for their silence, but most had no idea where the Jews were being taken and what the end result would be.

The Germans kept their insidious "Final Solution" secret. Adolf Hitler was hellbent on removing the Jews and other minorities, including Soviet prisoners of war. Initially, deportation was the proscribed method of getting rid of "undesirables." There was even talk of expelling Jews to faraway places like Siberia or Madagascar. When the concentration camps and ghettos that had been set up in Poland were being overloaded with detainees, the Nazis realized that mass deportations would be too costly. At the infamous Wannsee Conference on January 20th, 1942, the Nazis decided to employ their cynically titled "Final Solution."

They carried out a massive façade of carting Jewish people off to newly constructed concentration camps, where they were told they would work and live for the remainder of the war. The gates of Auschwitz even greeted them with the slogan "Arbeit Macht Frei" ("Work Makes One Free). These unfortunate souls were either sent to be gassed in the showers or forced to work under terrible conditions.

The Germans ordered Jewish camp inmates to take a "shower" for the purpose of delousing. The excuse was given that there was an outbreak of lice in the camps. The Jews were led into a room that looked like a large communal shower, complete with what looked like showerheads sticking out of the walls. They were made to stand under them, and the doors to the "shower room" (the gas chamber) were closed. The German guards outside would then turn on the gas. The victims were likely staring up at the faucets, fully expecting refreshing water to come out, only to be sprayed with poison gas. There was likely a terrible struggle as their lungs began to fail them, but it would not take long before the gas took its toll. Not all Jews perished in the gas chamber. Still, millions died in these horrible gas chambers.

The most glaring question of those who stumbled upon the aftermath of this horror show was, why? The answer is a complicated one, and it would likely take a whole book to even begin to come to grips with it.

First of all, one has to consider the historical precedents that existed before the Holocaust. The Jewish people have been historically persecuted for thousands of years. The Jews have often come into conflict with their neighbors over ideological differences. Judaism is a religion that calls for the nation of Israel to be holy and set apart.

When the Romans occupied the region, they found this stance a frustrating one. The Romans wished to spread the ideals of Greco-Roman culture over all the lands they occupied. When the Jews refused to act like the Romans, the two came into an ideological conflict.

After a series of Jewish revolts, the Roman legions poured in. The Romans destroyed the Jewish Temple in Jerusalem around the year 70 CE and dispersed the Jewish population. This was the start of the Jewish diaspora.

A Jewish sect known as Christians began spreading the gospel through the Roman Empire. The Roman Empire became Christian by the end of the 4th century. This spelled more problems for the Jewish diaspora, though, since Christians began to look at the Jews as not only heretics but as actively rejecting Christ.

One can only imagine the animosity that existed between Christians and Jews. Over the centuries, the Jewish diaspora in Christian Europe experienced both acceptance and hostility from their neighbors.

Adolf Hitler, for his part, hated both Jews and Christians. He kept his hatred of Christianity quiet since he knew that any move against the religion would not be feasible for him in the first phase of his plans for world domination. However, he went on the record with his associates to state that after the Jews were gone, he would come after the Christians next. In Hitler's mind, Christianity was an offshoot of Judaism, which weakened German morale. Hitler valued the Germanic values of the pagan past and preferred Odin, Thor, and Loki to the Father, the Son, and the Holy Spirit.

Hitler once stated, "Pure Christianity—the Christianity of the catacombs—is concerned with translating Christian doctrine into facts. It leads quite simply to the annihilation of mankind. It is wholehearted Bolshevism under a tinsel of metaphysics."[i] Hitler believed in survival of the fittest and despised anything that seemed to try to uplift the masses. He saw this as the "rotten branch of Christianity" at work.

Such things would have been shocking to everyday Germans, most of whom, despite their cowed silence, still considered themselves Christians. If known, it might have inspired them to stand up against Hitler and his Nazi henchmen. However, Hitler was crafty enough to keep these beliefs to himself. However, Hitler ultimately desired the eradication of anyone who did not share his views. To be clear, Adolf Hitler dreamed of a dystopian future in which everyone was firmly under the heel of the Nazi totalitarian boot. Fortunately for Germany and the rest of the world, that day never came.

---

[i] Spencer, Robert. *Religion of Peace?: Why Christianity Is and Islam Isn't.* 2007. Pg. 122.

Chapter 10: The Postwar and Cold War Era

"The smell of death overwhelmed us. More than 3,200 naked, emaciated bodies had been thrown into shallow graves. Others lay in the street where they had fallen. Lice crawled over the yellowed skin of their sharp, bony frames. I was too revolted to speak."

-General Omar Bradley[i]

On May 8th, 1945, the war in Europe officially came to an end. The United States and the Allies continued to fight Germany's former ally, Japan, for a few more months, but for Germany, it was over. And with the end of the war came quite a reckoning for the German people.

---

[i] O'Reilly Bill. *Hitler's Last Days: The Death of the Nazi Regime and the World's Most Notorious Dictator.* 2015. Pg. 292.

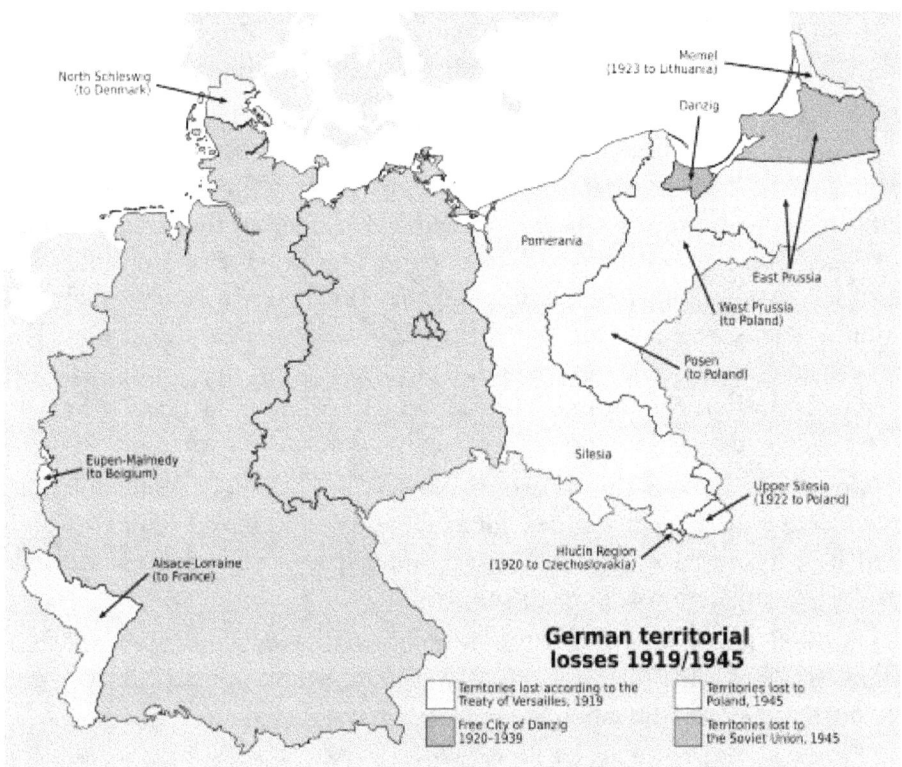

German territorial losses after both world wars.[12]

Germany was occupied by the Americans, British, and French in the west and the Russians in the east. Allied bombing in the later stages of the war had reduced most of Germany's cities to ruins and had killed an estimated 4.5 million Germans. Many of those Germans were civilians.

The defeated German survivors, as much as they had suffered, were in no position to condemn their conquerors. The vanquished had to look to those who had done the vanquishing for help as they clawed their way out of the wreckage that had been their homeland. They also had to come to grips with the fact that their nation was now a divided homeland.

The Germans found that some of the occupiers were more benign than others. The Soviets were more brutal. Fresh from the bloody and disturbing nightmare that had been the Eastern Front, the Russian troops were out for revenge. There are many accounts of Russians pouring into villages in East Germany, slaughtering men and raping women. The Russians also plundered and stole anything that might have been deemed valuable. Not all of this was spontaneous. Some of it was orchestrated. There were instances in which the Russians dismantled whole factories and sent them back east so that they could be repurposed and reinstalled in Russia.

The French, although not as bloodthirsty as the Russians, were also quite harsh, taking whatever they deemed fit. After the Americans admonished them, the French managed to stifle their feelings for revenge. The Americans reminded them of the Treaty of Versailles and let it be known that they did not want a repeat of the repercussions of punitive measures. No one wanted to deal with another world war. The Americans led the charge. They did not want to punish or destroy the Germans; rather, they wanted to rebuild the Allied-controlled sphere of West Germany so that it could eventually stand on its own.

Communism and the Western nations' increasingly chilly relations with the Soviet Union loomed large. The West realized it was in their own best interest to make West Germany strong enough to stand as a bulwark against encroaching communism.

The US led the way with this rebuilding of Germany by way of the Marshall Plan. This plan was a four-year initiative to inject resources into war-torn Western Europe.

The Soviets had plans of their own. In 1946, they helped establish a communist government in East Germany with the Socialist Union Party at the helm.

Both America and its allies, as well as the Soviets, had difficulty figuring out what to do with former Nazis. It seemed like common sense to just get rid of them all. However, upon further looking into the matter, the occupiers discovered there was a big difference between "nominal" Nazis and "real" Nazis. Toward the end of the Nazi regime, just about anyone who wanted to do anything by way of a professional career had to join the Nazi Party. These people did not necessarily join the party because they agreed with Nazi ideology; they only did so to get a job. It was for this reason that countless doctors, dentists, and construction workers were card-carrying Nazis. The occupiers had to learn not to worry so much about who was a party member (since most of the country was) but those who played a distinct role in the regime. After all, there was a big difference between a guy who worked every day of his life as a dentist and Heinrich Himmler, who was the head of the SS.

On May 23rd, 1949, the Western nations merged their three occupation zones together to establish the Federal Republic of West

Germany. Germany was now clearly split between West and East.

The capital of West Germany was Bonn. Perhaps the most troubling part of this arrangement was the fact that the old German capital of Berlin, although well within the Soviet zone of influence, was split between the Allies and the Soviets. This created immense problems when the Soviets decided to shut off access to West Belin. Many retellings of this history give the impression that the Soviets did such a thing for no reason. It was as if they were just flexing their muscle and testing the resolve of the West. But what many retellings gloss over is the triggering event that led the Soviets to act.

The Western Allies had minted a new currency, German marks, in West Germany and West Berlin. The Soviets had created a different currency for the East Berliners. The trouble began when the Western-backed currency deposited in West Berlin began to circulate in East Berlin. This created a severe disruption among the East Berliners and outraged the Soviets, who viewed it as a trespass against previous agreements the West had made not to interfere with East Berlin. This incident led the Soviets to take the arguably drastic step of blockading the roads to West Berlin.

This act led to the Berlin Airlift, which was conducted between 1948 and 1949. This was an ingenious and daring air relief program in which the Americans and the British dropped packages of food, coal, and other necessities to the citizens of West Berlin from airplanes. The Soviets could shut down the roads, but they could not close the skies. They were unable to completely stop the flow of goods.

Germans watching a US plane fly in with supplies during the Berlin Airlift.[18]

Realizing it was pointless, the Soviets agreed to lift the blockade. However, they would not give up on the idea of cutting East Berlin off from the West, and the Soviets continued to tighten their grip.

In 1955, East Germany was made an official part of the Warsaw Pact, which held the Eastern Bloc of communist states together. East Germany, which the communists had dubbed the German Democratic Republic, had become the front line in the Cold War. The lines were now clearly drawn between the Western and Eastern blocs. Adding to this was a menacing set of barbed wire that was placed across the border regions.

At this point, East and West Berlin were still open to traffic, but the obvious intention of making these border crossings more difficult led to an ever-increasing flood of East Berliners to the West. In 1961, in an effort to prevent Western meddling and to stave the flow of migrants from East Berlin to West Berlin, the communists began to construct a massive wall. The Berlin Wall, as it would be known, was a massive stretch of concrete. This wall was erected to effectively cut off East Berlin from West Berlin. There were several checkpoints along the wall, and armed soldiers watched to make sure no one tried to climb or otherwise penetrate this barrier.

On the other side of that wall, things were going far differently. In the late 1950s, West Germany experienced an economic boon known as the Wirtschaftswunder. The term roughly translates into English as "economic miracle." Why was it a miracle? Well, after being bombed during the war, West Germany was able to rebuild industrial plants, ramp up production, export products, and see huge economic growth. The year 1958 saw West Germany enter into the European Economic Community (the EEC), a precursor of what would ultimately become the European Union.

Those in charge of the German Democratic Republic (GDR) feared that East Germany might be left in West Germany's dust. Communist planners in 1963 enacted the New Economic System, a series of reforms designed to allow some decentralization from what had otherwise been a command economy. It also gave more control to the skilled technocrats, who were charged with running the most vital operations of the GDR.

These reforms improved the economy of the GDR for some time, with exceptional growth occurring by the 1970s. It was good while it lasted, but the bottom would eventually fall out.

Change was on its way. In 1971, German politician Erich Honecker rose to prominence as the general secretary of East Germany's communist party. Honecker wished to present himself as a party man, but he found himself being drawn into international unrest. In 1975, claims of human rights abuse led to the landmark Helsinki Declaration, which sought to give some basic guarantee of human rights in the Eastern Bloc—East Germany included. Such reforms stood in stark contrast to the Berlin Wall and the dreaded Stasi, the German secret police who watched everything that the East Germans did.

The East Germans increasingly longed to be reunited with the West. They embraced Western culture, just as they embraced news broadcasts that came from West Germany. As much as the communists wished to build walls and barriers, they could not stop broadcast TV signals!

In 1985, the new leader of the Soviet Union, Mikhail Gorbachev, began openly speaking of reform within the Soviet Union and its Eastern Bloc satellite states. He spoke of both glasnost ("openness") and perestroika ("reforming"). These were the two things that East Germans craved the most: governmental reform and the commitment to a more transparent and open society.

This openness allowed for more discussions about and even protests against the current conditions in East Germany. An increasingly bold public began to actively push back against the restrictions they had lived under, especially against the most visible symbol of their repression, the Berlin Wall.

Berliners greeted US President Ronald Reagan with cheers at the Brandenburg Gate in 1987. Reagan famously demanded, "Mr. Gorbachev, tear down this wall!" A couple of years later, the Germans helped Mr. Gorbachev do just that. On November 9th, 1989, both East and West Germans came together to dismantle the wall. This act was encouraged by guards who opened the gates and allowed citizens to pass back and forth. Even as an increasingly unruly crowd climbed and stood on top of the wall, the guards made it clear there would be no repercussions.

Seemingly given the green light, Germans began to use whatever they could, whether hammers or their bare hands, to tear down the Berlin Wall. The Soviets and their communist enforcers practically did nothing to stop this event from unfolding. Both the end of the Cold War and the reunification of Germany finally seemed near.

Chapter 11: Reunification and Beyond: Modern Germany

The Berlin Wall came crashing down in 1989. The following year, the country would officially come together as one. As cries of "Wir sind ein Volk!" (or as it would be rendered in English, "We are one people!") filled the air, Germans demanded that the previously fractured halves of their nation be put back together.

No one thought this would be an easy task, yet it was actually far easier than anyone imagined it would be. With just a stroke of a pen, on October 3rd, 1990, the reunification of Germany was made a reality. With this treaty, the German Democratic Republic was dismantled, and East Germany was absorbed into West Germany's federal republic. The capital of unified Germany would move from Bonn back to the traditional capital of Berlin.

These things were accomplished under West German Chancellor Helmut Kohl. Kohl was a charismatic and robust politician who set out on an ambitious ten-point program, which outlined the path forward for the full integration of the two halves of Germany into one nation.

Kohl was first elected in West Germany in 1982, and it was under his watch that the Berlin Wall fell in 1989 and the two halves were united in 1990. In fact, Kohl won his reelection in 1990 on the pledge to make sure that Germany was reunited sooner rather than later.

Once unification began, it was clear that East Germany had some catching up to do in order to match the industrial might and economic power of West Germany. Some outsiders voiced reservations about a united and stronger Germany. *Time* magazine even published a piece shortly after unification, openly asking if the world should be cautious in reviving a Germany that had previously instigated two global conflicts.

After the ecstatic joy of tearing down the wall and reunifying had died down, the Germans themselves began to question such things. Moreover, the Germans began to question their own identity. Who were they? And how could they rise above the guilt of their past? The West Germans had long ago begged for forgiveness for the past crimes of the Nazis. West Germany had been paying hefty reparations to Israel. It was a small consolation when compared to the horrors of the Holocaust, but it was at least an effort.

The East Germans had never really confronted their past. After the war, the communists, seeking to bolster East German morale against the West, twisted the narrative by insisting that the Nazis were an offshoot of capitalism. The East Germans were raised to believe that by becoming communists, they had distanced themselves from the Nazis. To this day, it is said that West Germans are more likely to be more apologetic about past atrocities even if they had not been born at the time they occurred than East Germans would. East Germans are also said to be more easygoing and more likely to fully embrace being German.

Helmut Kohl seemed eager to reassure the world that Germany had moved past the old sense of nationalism in favor of a more globalist stance. Germany's inroads in the nascent European Union (EU) seemed to back up such claims. In 1993, the EU as we know it today came into being through the Maastricht Treaty. This treaty sought to dissolve some aspects of national distinction in favor of universal citizenship within the EU. For many Germans eager to shed the guilt of the past and for those who felt too disconnected to even associate with it, this likely seemed to be the best and most logical step forward.

Kohl remained in office until 1998, when his successor, Gerhard Schröder, was elected. Gerhard positioned himself as a moderate. He was neither too liberal nor too conservative. Under Gerhard, Germany entered the Eurozone by officially adopting the EU currency (the euro) as legal tender. Gerhard stayed in office until 2005 when Angela Merkel was elected.

Merkel would have to deal with the Eurozone crisis that erupted during the Great Recession of 2008. While other EU countries faltered,

Germany remained strong. In fact, it was strong enough to repeatedly bail other EU members out. One of the newest additions to the EU, Greece, has been a major recipient of German aid.

The fact that Greece ended up owing Germany so much money in bailout loans would later create much resentment among the Greeks. This resentment came to a head in 2015 when Greece's prime minister, Alexis Tsipras, began to suggest that it should not be Greece paying Germany but rather Germany paying Greece. This was in light of a new push to get Germany to pay reparations for its part in invading and occupying Greece in the Second World War. Such things were not very popular with the German public, who felt as if they had already done more than enough since the war's end in 1945.

Such discussions were still underway when Germany and much of the rest of the world were rocked by a global pandemic. Germany experienced its first cases as early as January 2020.

Angela Merkel's response was to immediately send the nation into lockdown to prevent further spread of the disease. However, this had a dire effect on the economy since it meant no one was working. Disaffection with these results saw Angela Merkel make her exit after sixteen years of leadership. She was replaced by a more liberal politician, Olaf Scholz.

Since becoming chancellor, the greatest issue that Scholz has faced so far is the Russian invasion of Ukraine, which occurred in February 2022. Germany, along with the rest of the EU, Britain, and the United States, has been a strong supporter of Ukraine in its struggle against Russia.

Along with opening their wallets, Germans have also opened their doors, allowing over a million refugees from Ukraine, Syria, and other countries. During the first half of the 20th century, no one imagined Germany being such a welcoming place, but so far, the first few decades of the 21st century have changed that opinion considerably.

Conclusion

It is common for nations around the world to embrace some form of patriotism, some sense of nationalism. Americans sing the anthem "The Star-Spangled Banner" and the British proudly fly the Union Jack. Germans have long sought to have some sort of national identity. However, their quest for national recognition has been exceedingly difficult and is usually flummoxed by the preconceived notions of outsiders.

At the beginning of Germany's recorded history, the Romans noted a distinct culture and even attitude among the warring tribes of Central Europe. Roman observers admired not only the martial prowess of these warriors but also their sense of honor. The warriors seemed to have deep respect for family and tribal bonds. Such things, on a much smaller scale, form the very core of national identity. A nation of people could be said to be essentially one giant extended family of shared laws, customs, and values.

The Franks, which historians also link with French history, saw their warrior king, Clovis, attempt to make himself a new Roman emperor. Charlemagne the Great would prove successful at this task, being officially crowned as such in 800 CE by the pope. This kickstarted the Holy Roman Empire, a conglomeration of states in Central Europe so confusing and confounding that it provided excellent fodder for French satirist Voltaire. He joked that the realm was not really an empire. Roman, or holy!

After the Holy Roman Empire's dissolution, thanks to the actions of Napoleon Bonaparte, Prussia and Austria rose to prominence. These were both German-speaking realms, but the sense of nationalism in both were quite different. Rather than nationalism, both trended to embrace cosmopolitanism. However, when Prussia seized the rest of the German states in the west and forged its Reich (or empire), a long-dormant sense of German nationalism arose.

This sense of Germany's unique place in the world was nurtured during and after World War One. It then rose its ugly head in a horrific way during World War Two. After this nightmare came to a close, many, both outside and inside Germany, started saying, "Never again." And for most, the answer to never having such terrible things occur on German soil was to get rid of any sense of German identity.

It is for this reason that Germans today are more likely to shy away from the idea of nationalism. For them, the term "nationalist" is almost akin to a derogatory word. Germans, for the most part, want to embrace international globalism, multinational parties, and being part of supernational organizations like the European Union.

It has been a hard road for the denizens of Central Europe who aspire to take part in what amounts to a post-German society. But hopefully, as they travel down this difficult, winding path, this nation will find a much brighter and more meaningful future.

Here's another book by Enthralling History that you might like

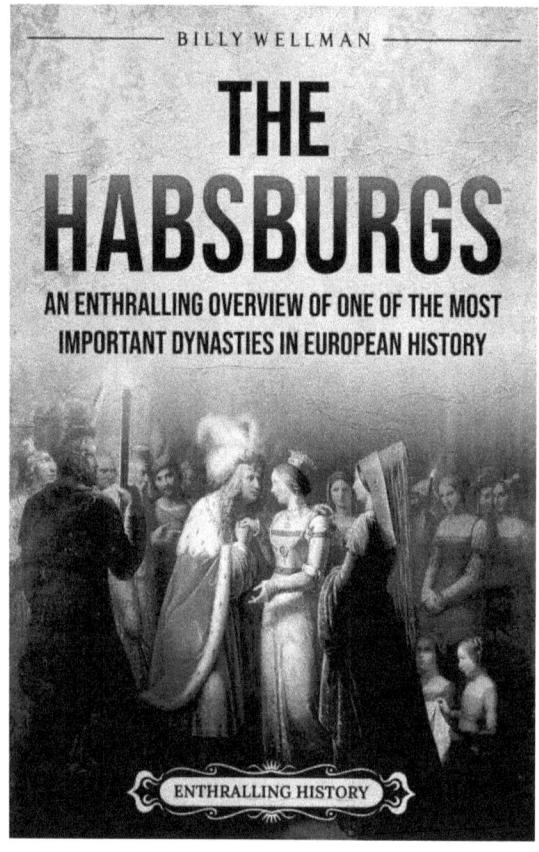

Free limited time bonus

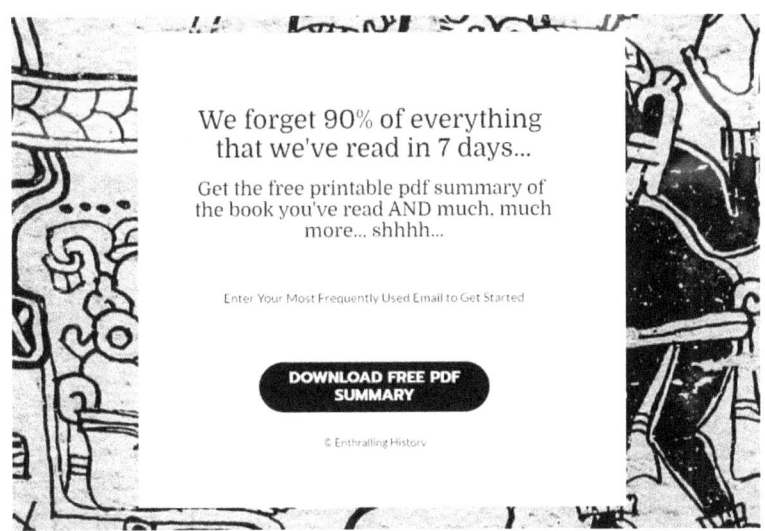

Stop for a moment. We have a free bonus set up for you. The problem is this: we forget 90% of everything that we read after 7 days. Crazy fact, right? Here's the solution: we've created a printable, 1-page pdf summary for this book that you're reading now. All you have to do to get your free pdf summary is to go to the following website: https://livetolearn.lpages.co/enthrallinghistory/

Or, Scan the QR code!

Once you do, it will be intuitive. Enjoy, and thank you!

Further Reading and Reference

Coy, Jason Philip. *A Brief History of Germany*. 2010.

Detwiler, Donald. *Germany: A Short History*. 1976.

Ozment, Steven. *A Mighty Fortress*. 2004.

Benjamin G., Craig. *The Big History of Civilizations*. 2016.

Murray, V. *The Crusades: An Encyclopedia*. 2006.

McGiffert, Cushman. *Martin Luther: The Man and His Work*. 1911.

Gibson, Andrew. *Modernity and the Political Fix*. 2019.

Spencer, Robert. *Religion of Peace?: Why Christianity Is and Islam Isn't*. 2007.

McCabe, Joseph. *A History of the Popes*. 1939.

Middleton, John. *World Monarchies and Dynasties*. 2005.

Pelican, Jaroslav. *Credo: Historical and Theological Guide to Creeds and Confessions of Faith*. 2014.

O'Reilly Bill. *Hitler's Last Days: The Death of the Nazi Regime and the World's Most Notorious Dictator*. 2015.

Retallack, James. *Imperial Germany: 1871-1918*. 2008.

The New English Bible with the Apocrypha. 1970.

Image Sources

[1] *Bullenwächter, CC BY 3.0 <https://creativecommons.org/licenses/by/3.0>, via Wikimedia Commons; https://commons.wikimedia.org/wiki/File:Bronze_figure_of_a_German_Biblioth%C3%A8que_Nationale.jpg*

[2] *User:MapMaster, CC BY-SA 2.5 <https://creativecommons.org/licenses/by-sa/2.5>, via Wikimedia Commons; https://commons.wikimedia.org/wiki/File:Invasions_of_the_Roman_Empire_1.png*

[3] *Blank map of Europe.svg: maix₡?derivative work: Alphathon, CC BY-SA 4.0 <https://creativecommons.org/licenses/by-sa/4.0>, via Wikimedia Commons; https://commons.wikimedia.org/wiki/File:Francia_814.svg*

[4] *Holy Roman Empire 1000 map-fr.svg: Sémhurderivative work: OwenBlacker / Discussion, CC BY-SA 3.0 <https://creativecommons.org/licenses/by-sa/3.0>, via Wikimedia Commons; https://commons.wikimedia.org/wiki/File:Holy_Roman_Empire_11th_century_map-en.svg*

[5] *https://commons.wikimedia.org/wiki/File:Friedrich_I._Barbarossa.jpg*

[6] *https://commons.wikimedia.org/wiki/File:Peter_Janssen,_Kaiser_Friedrich_II.jpg*

[7] *https://commons.wikimedia.org/wiki/File:Luther_at_the_Diet_of_Worms.jpg*

[8] *Map_Thirty_Years_War-fr.svg: historicairderivative work: P. S. Burton, CC BY-SA 2.5 <https://creativecommons.org/licenses/by-sa/2.5>, via Wikimedia Commons; https://commons.wikimedia.org/wiki/File:Map_Thirty_Years_War-en.svg*

[9] *https://commons.wikimedia.org/wiki/File:Friedrich_der_Gro%C3%9Fe_(1781_or_1786)_-_Google_Art_Project.jpg*

[10] *Deutsches_Reich1.png: kgbergerderivative work: Wiggy!, CC BY-SA 2.5 <https://creativecommons.org/licenses/by-sa/2.5>, via Wikimedia Commons; https://commons.wikimedia.org/wiki/File:Deutsches_Reich_(1871-1918)-en.png*

[11] *Goran tek-en, CC BY-SA 4.0 <https://creativecommons.org/licenses/by-sa/4.0>, via Wikimedia*

Commons; https://commons.wikimedia.org/wiki/File:World_War_II_in_Europe,_1942.svg

[12] *Aeroid, CC BY-SA 4.0 <https://creativecommons.org/licenses/by-sa/4.0>, via Wikimedia Commons; https://commons.wikimedia.org/wiki/File:German_territorial_losses_1919_and_1945.svg*

[13] https://commons.wikimedia.org/wiki/File:C-54landingattemplehof.jpg

www.ingramcontent.com/pod-product-compliance
Lightning Source LLC
Chambersburg PA
CBHW070341010526
44107CB00004B/576